The Image
of Their
Greatness

Other Books by the Authors

BY LAWRENCE RITTER

The Glory of Their Times

BY DONALD HONIG

Baseball When the Grass Was Real

Baseball Between the Lines

The Man in the Dugout

The October Heroes

The Image
of Their
Greatness

An Illustrated History of Baseball
from 1900 to the Present

LAWRENCE RITTER and DONALD HONIG

Crown Publishers, Inc. New York

Inquiries should be addressed to Crown Publishers, Inc.,
One Park Avenue, New York, N.Y. 10016

Published simultaneously in Canada by General Publishing Company
Limited

Printed in the United States of America

Library of Congress Cataloging in Publication Data

Ritter, Lawrence S
 The image of their greatness.

 Includes index.
 1. Baseball—United States—History. I. Honig, Donald, joint author. II. Title.
GV863.AIR56 1979   796.357'0973   78-27004
ISBN 0-517-53625-0

FOR STEVE RITTER AND CATHERINE HONIG
SON AND DAUGHTER
WITH LOVE

Contents

Time is of the essence. The shadow moves
From the plate to the box, from the box to second base,
From second to the outfield, to the bleachers.

Time is of the essence. The crowd and players
Are the same age always, but the man in the crowd
Is older every season. Come on, play ball!

—From "Polo Grounds"
by Rolfe Humphries

Preface

THIS is an illustrated history of baseball from the turn of the century to the present. The camera has always been an adjunct to baseball, ever since the days when a few thousand derby-hatted spectators, almost all male, sat in ramshackle wooden grandstands and watched young men named Mathewson, Wagner, and Cobb set standards for future generations. From the outset the camera was there, on the field, in the dugout, recording the astonishing growth of a sweet and simple game into a tremendous industry, acted out now in magnificent temples before millions of worshipers throughout the length and breadth of the land.

The camera captures and holds forever the heroes of childhood, the memories of youth. It seizes and holds forever their swings and their throws, their smiles and their frowns, their slides into clouds of dust that have yet to settle. History tells us that Mathewson, Wagner, Cobb, and Ruth grew old; that DiMaggio became silver-haired and Williams mellow; and that even those most recent of prodigies, Mays and Mantle, have begun to show the weather in their faces.

But none of this is true, as this book bears witness. Mathewson, Wagner, and Cobb rise with the turn of a page to dominate a generation; Ruth's magic remains poetically pure; and DiMaggio, Williams, Mays, and Mantle continue to drive baseballs into dots against the sky and to move across the outfield grass with grace and fury.

Time is of the essence. The camera catches yesterday, holds it until tomorrow. Within these pages time, for a moment, stands still.

LAWRENCE S. RITTER
DONALD HONIG
1979

The Early Years
1900-1909

JOHN JOSEPH MCGRAW was a small-town boy who made it big as a runty 120-pound third baseman with the rough and tough Baltimore Orioles in the 1890s. In 1902, at the age of twenty-nine, he was appointed manager of the last-place New York Giants, and in the next dozen years he clawed his way to five pennants and narrowly missed another. In subsequent years he argued, bullied, and schemed his way to five more.

John McGraw and Ty Cobb were the dominant figures in the sporting life of this country for the first two decades of the twentieth century, and they were more than a little alike. Both scratched and scrounged for whatever they could wrest from a harsh environment inhabited by hostile legions. And both were essentially humorless men—although, to tell the truth, McGraw, unlike Cobb, often appeared to be having some trouble suppressing a twinkle in his eye, especially in his younger days. Many of McGraw's players hated his tyrannical ways, but more loved him and almost all admired him. He was a martinet, capable of lashing verbal abuse, but when his guard was down and he thought no one was looking, he often revealed a surprising warmth and compassion and a generous tolerance for human weakness.

John J. McGraw.
Manager, New York Giants,
1902-1932.

Manager McGraw tolerated no back talk and quickly traded away players who resisted his absolute authority. But he never

O   1

traded moody, independent Bill Terry, the best first baseman in the league, who refused to knuckle under from the start. And on June 3, 1932, he summoned Terry to his office, told him to close the door—the first words he had spoken to him in weeks—and asked, "How would you like to replace me as manager of this ball club?"

McGraw's personality was so complex, so full of contradictions, that one cannot help probing its genesis. One wonders what scars were left by the death, when he was twelve, of his mother, two brothers, and two sisters, all victims of a diphtheria epidemic. Later his first wife died, in 1899, after but two years of marriage. He was childless and some of his players became surrogate sons, but his two special favorites died young—pitcher Christy Mathewson and outfielder Ross Youngs. Mathewson died of tuberculosis at the age of forty-five, and Youngs of Bright's disease at the height of his career, only thirty years of age.

McGraw managed the Giants for thirty tumultuous years, and when he retired in favor of Terry, in 1932, he was still as pugnacious as when he had first arrived in New York. But he was lonelier. And baseball, New York, and America itself had changed from under him. Two years later he died. The medical report said the cause was uremia, but those who were closest to him knew that it was mostly because John J. McGraw was no longer top dog.

The rise and early career of John McGraw coincided with the rise and early growth of baseball in this country. He was born in poverty in upstate New York in 1873, when baseball was just learning to crawl, and began his managerial career at the turn of the century, when baseball was starting to come of age. For modern baseball, as we know it today, dates from as recently as around the turn of the century.

It is true that the first professional baseball team, the Cincinnati Red Stockings, toured the country soon after the Civil War, and that the National League was organized shortly thereafter, in 1876. But it was a different game then. Pitchers threw underhand; it took nine balls (rather than four) for a batter to get a base on balls; and the pitching distance was only 45 feet. It was 1884 before pitchers were allowed to throw overhand, 1889 before four balls entitled a batter to walk to first base, and 1893 before the pitching distance was lengthened to the present 60 feet 6 inches. By the turn of the century, however, the playing rules had evolved to about the same as today's.

At roughly the same time—in 1901, to be exact—the American League was organized, creating, along with the National League, the basic structure of major league baseball that remains to this day. For a while relations between the two leagues were

Tyrus Raymond Cobb. Lifetime batting average: .367.

strained, as the owners argued about territorial rights and player contracts and threatened to sue each other into extinction. A World Series—the first—was played between the National and American League pennant winners at the end of the 1903 season, with the National League's Pittsburgh Pirates succumbing to the new league's Boston Pilgrims (they were not called the Red Sox until 1907). But there was no similar series the following year because McGraw's pennant-winning New York Giants flatly refused to meet the American League's champions.

Soon the dust settled, however; officials of the two leagues came to terms with each other, and cooperation replaced conflict.

An overflow crowd tries to catch a glimpse of the 1905 World Series at New York's Polo Grounds.

Christy Mathewson in 1901.

Christy Mathewson warming up (about 1905).

Postseason competition was resumed in 1905. With playing rules stabilized and interleague disputes resolved, baseball was on its way: within a remarkably short time it had captured the nation's imagination and become America's undisputed National Pastime!

The opposing managers in the 1905 World Series were the New York Giants' John McGraw and the Philadelphia Athletics' Cornelius McGillicuddy, better known as Connie Mack. They were a study in opposites. McGraw, short, fiery, belligerent, former star third baseman, chewed barbed wire for breakfast and umpires for a midday snack. Mack, tall, thin as a beanpole, even-tempered, mild-mannered, former journeyman catcher, was as much a father to his players as their manager. If virtue were to triumph, it would have to be Connie Mack hands down. But it was a World Series, not Judgment Day, and the Giants had Christy Mathewson's right arm on their side. With Mathewson pitching three shutouts, the Giants overpowered the Athletics four games to one.

Over a period of six days, Mathewson won the first, third, and fifth games by scores of 3-0, 9-0, and 2-0, allowing a total of only 14 hits. Iron Man Joe McGinnity won the other game for the Giants, 1-0. The Iron Man had become famous by pitching both halves of doubleheaders, a feat he performed on five different occasions—three times winning both games of the doubleheader. Philadelphia's only victory came in the second game when Chief Bender, an imposing Chippewa from Carlisle Indian School and Dickinson College, blanked the Giants, 3-0. Thus the 1905 World Series remains unique in history, with five shutouts in five games.

One reason the Athletics lost is that ace pitcher Rube Waddell injured his shoulder in a friendly scuffle with a teammate before the Series started. Waddell was one of the most colorful as well as the most effective pitchers of his day. His reputation as an eccentric was established early in his career when he used to pour ice water on his pitching arm between innings. "That's to slow me down a little," he'd say. "I've got so much speed I'll burn up the catcher's mitt if I don't cool off a bit."

In many respects the 1905 Series was a watershed in the history of the game. Until then, professional baseball had an unsavory reputation as a rowdy sport, played mainly by roughnecks and more often than not interrupted by bickering and fistfights, off the field as well as on. Young men would think twice before taking their best girl to see a professional ball game. But when the 1905 Series opened, Eddie Plank, a product of Gettysburg College, was on the pitching mound for the Athletics, and young Christy Mathewson, from Bucknell University, was the starting pitcher for the Giants.

Roger Bresnahan, Matty's catcher from 1905 through 1908. Bresnahan was the first catcher to wear shin guards, donning them to hoots of derision in 1907.

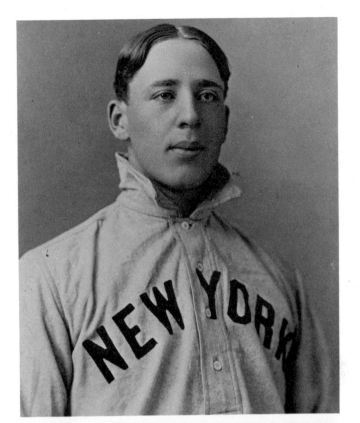

Leon "Red" Ames, Giants'
pitcher from 1903 to 1913
and with other National
League teams through
1919. Ames was a 22-game
winner for John McGraw in
1905.

Rube Waddell (about 1906).
One of the greatest (and
most eccentric) left-handers of all time. From 1900
through 1907 he led the
league in strikeouts seven
times.

Connie Mack with three of his top pitchers: **left to right**, Jack Coombs, Eddie Plank, and Boardwalk Brown.

Charles Albert "Chief"
Bender, a Chippewa from
Carlisle Indian School and
Dickinson College, and
Connie Mack's star right-
hander from 1903 through
1914.

An early photograph of pitcher Eddie Plank sitting next to the Philadelphia Athletics' dugout. Plank won 20 or more games eight times, over 300 lifetime from 1901 through 1917.

It was Christy Mathewson, more than anyone, who changed the public image of the game and elevated it into the mainstream of American life. Matty symbolized the ideal All-American Boy: handsome, well educated, reserved, the embodiment of middle-class conduct and values, as well as a superb all-around athlete and the outstanding pitcher of his generation. Born in Factoryville, Pennsylvania, the son of well-to-do parents, he played football in addition to baseball at Bucknell. He was also a member of the glee club and the literary society, and was elected class president.

Mathewson joined the Giants in 1900, and with his famous "fadeaway" (today it would be called a screwball) was soon a 20- and then a 30-game winner. In 1903, '04, and '05 he won 30, 33, and 31 games respectively, on his way to an amazing 37 victories in 1908. Few pitchers have been his equal, before or since, and surely none, with the possible exception of Walter Johnson, has received the overwhelming adulation that was showered on Matty for his behavior off the field as well as on.

"He is a good man, a very good man," his wife once said, vainly trying to reduce him to human proportions, "but he is not a goody-goody."

McGraw—or Muggsy as he was often called, but never to his face—hardly had time to enjoy his 1905 World Series victory before he found himself cast in the role of an also-ran. The Chicago Cubs, managed by their young first baseman, Frank Chance—the "Peerless Leader"—finished on top in the National League in four of the next five seasons. The glory years in all the annals of the Chicago Cubs are still those years, 1906 through 1910, when they won four pennants and two World Championships. The Cubs have won a number of pennants since then, but never again two in a row, not to mention three.

Bill Klem, circa 1906. Klem umpired in the National League from 1905 through 1940 and is generally considered the greatest umpire of all time.

Mordecai "Three-Fingered" Brown, six consecutive years a 20-game winner for the Chicago Cubs (from 1906 through 1911).

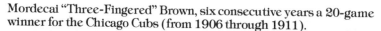

→ **Left to right:** Christy Mathewson, John McGraw, and "Iron Man" Joe McGinnity in 1903. Five times Joe McGinnity pitched both halves of doubleheaders, on three occasions winning both games. He pitched in the major and minor leagues for 33 years, from 1893 through 1925; in 1925, at the age of 54, his record was 6 wins and 6 losses with Dubuque of the Mississippi Valley League.

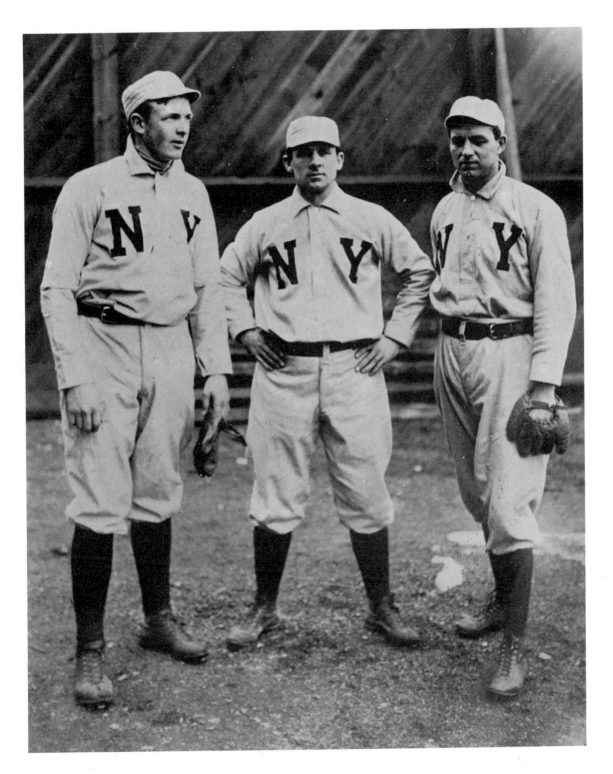

Shortstop Joe Tinker.

Second baseman Johnny
Evers.

First baseman Frank
Chance, the Peerless Leader.

Orvie Overall, twice a 20-game winner for the Cubs (in 1907 and 1909).

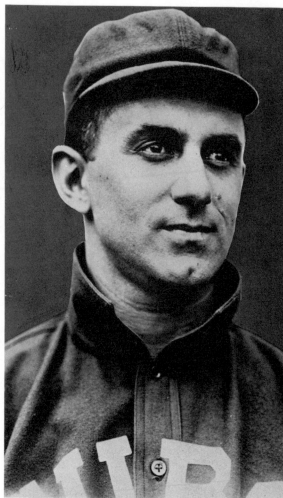

Ed Reulbach won 20 games and lost only 4 for the Cubs in 1906, and won 24 with just 7 losses in 1908.

Left fielder Jimmy Sheckard, a regular in the Cubs' outfield from 1906 through 1912.

→ Big Ed Walsh of the White Sox. In 1908 he won 40 games.

Cubs' shortstop Joe Tinker, **left,** and White Sox manager and center
fielder Fielder Jones, shortly before the start of the 1906 World Series.

Jimmy Collins of the Boston Americans (now the Red Sox). In the early years of the century he was considered the finest fielding third baseman in the game.

Elmer Flick, star Cleveland outfielder from 1902 through 1910.

Those were the years of Tinker to Evers to Chance, the most fabled double-play combination of all time, and of Mordecai "Three-Fingered" Brown, one of the few pitchers able to beat the great Mathewson. They frequently opposed each other over the years, often in crucial games, with Three-Fingered Brown winning 13 of 24 decisions. Harry Steinfeldt completed the Chicago infield at third base, and Johnny Kling and Jimmy Archer shared the catching. In the outfield were Wildfire Schulte, Solly Hofman, Jimmy Sheckard, and Jimmy Slagle. And joining Three-Fingered Brown on the pitching staff were Orvie Overall, Ed Reulbach, and Jack Pfiester.

Frank Chance became manager of the Chicago Cubs in 1905, when he was but twenty-seven years old. A 190-pound 6-footer, he had been attending Washington College in Irvington, California, planning to become a doctor, when an opportunity arose to try out with the Cubs in 1898. He made the club as second-string catcher—never playing a day in the minors—and came into his own when he was shifted to first base several years later. His intelligence and leadership qualities were so obvious that it was no surprise when he was appointed playing manager after having been a regular only two years.

Joe Tinker, the shortstop, and Johnny Evers, second baseman, worked so smoothly together, and became so famous for executing double plays, that the expression "from Tinker to Evers to Chance" became a part of the language. Actually, their double-play skills were probably overrated, much of their fame coming from a lament written by newspaper columnist Franklin P. Adams, a dyed-in-the-wool Giant fan. It began:

> These are the saddest of possible words—
> Tinker to Evers to Chance.
> Trio of Bear Cubs and fleeter than birds—
> Tinker to Evers to Chance.

Off the field, Tinker and Evers had little mutual affection and rarely spoke to each other. The scrappy little Evers—whose playing weight was well under 150 pounds—wasn't much of a talker to begin with. He spent most of his time reading the Official Baseball Rules and **The Sporting News**, a policy that paid off when his quick thinking precipitated the famous "Merkle incident" near the end of the 1908 season.

Mordecai Peter Centennial "Three-Fingered" Brown—his parents threw in the extra middle name because he was born in 1876—was a farm boy from Indiana who joined the Cubs in 1904 and proceeded to win 20 or more games every season from 1906

Catcher Johnny Kling, Chicago Cubs' mainstay from 1900 through 1910.

Ed Walsh, **left**, and Addie Joss in 1908. Joss won 20 or more games for Cleveland four years in a row (1905 through 1908), including a perfect game in 1908 in which he beat Walsh 1-0. Three years later, however, he died of tubercular meningitis at the age of thirty-one.

Jack Chesbro, 41-game winner for the New York Highlanders (now the Yankees) in 1904. This is still the American League record for most victories in a season.

Ty Cobb.

Ty Cobb.

Cobb sliding into third against the Highlanders (the third baseman is
Jimmy Austin).

Cobb rounding a base.

Cobb batting.

Sam Crawford, hard-hitting Detroit outfielder from 1903 through 1917. His 312 lifetime triples have never been approached.

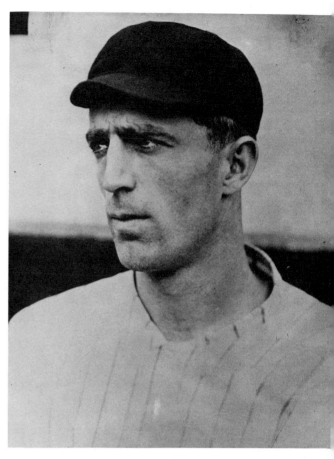

Al Bridwell, New York Giants' shortstop, in 1908— the man who sent Fred Merkle on his way.

Fred Merkle.

through 1911. As a youngster he had an accident with some farm equipment, which resulted in the amputation of most of the index finger on his right hand (his throwing hand). The same accident also rendered the little finger of that hand useless. Nevertheless, his pitching hardly suffered; indeed, he always claimed it gave his sinker ball that something extra no one else could duplicate.

Strictly on the record, Frank Chance's 1906 Chicago Cubs have a claim to being the greatest team of all time. They won 116 games that season, on their way to the first of three successive pennants, and lost only 36. No other team has ever done as well. (By comparison, the 1954 Cleveland Indians won 111 games, the 1927 Yankees 110, the 1975 Cincinnati Reds 108, and the 1929 Philadelphia Athletics "only" 104.) However, to everyone's astonishment the Cubs lost the World Series in six games to their crosstown rivals, the Chicago White Sox—the "Hitless Wonders."

The 1906 White Sox were known as the Hitless Wonders for

good reason. They had a team batting average of only .230, lowest in the league, with not a single regular hitting as high as .280. Their manager, who also played center field, had the wonderful name of Fielder Jones—his real name, not a nickname—and, needless to say, he had to have some very good pitchers just to stay afloat, much less win the pennant. And he had them: mainly Doc White, a topnotch left-hander; Nick Altrock and Frank Owen, both 20-game winners; and Big Ed Walsh, whose spitball was a sight to behold.

Thinking back about Ed Walsh's spitball, an opposing player once recalled, "I think the ball disintegrated on the way to the plate and the catcher put it back together again; I swear, when it went past the plate it was just the spit went by."

This pitching staff, plus a splurge of totally unexpected World Series base hits, was enough to enable the White Sox to beat the Cubs—in all respects apparently the better team—in one of the biggest upsets in World Series history.

But in the larger scheme of things it was only a temporary setback for Frank Chance's Cubs, and probably a fluke, because in the next two years—1907 and 1908—the Cubs won the National League pennant and the World Series, while the White Sox, after their surprising triumph, sank lower and lower in the American League standings and didn't win another pennant until 1917. One reason they didn't repeat is that a skinny nineteen-year-old started playing regularly in the Detroit Tigers' outfield in 1906 and, led by his phenomenal hitting and baserunning, the Tigers won three straight American League pennants in 1907, 1908, and 1909.

The youngster's name was Tyrus Raymond Cobb, the "Georgia Peach," and he is generally acknowledged to be one of the greatest baseball players who ever lived, if not the greatest. (His only rivals for that exalted honor are Babe Ruth and perhaps Honus Wagner.) Ty Cobb's batting feats are almost beyond belief: three times he hit over .400; twelve times he led the league in batting, amassing 4,191 hits over his career (no one else has even reached 4,000); and, most impressive of all, his lifetime batting average was .367. Few players have maintained as high an average for a single season; Cobb did it over 24 seasons, stretching from 1905 through 1928. And on the base paths he was a whirlwind: he stole 892 bases lifetime (the record until broken by Lou Brock in 1977), including 96 in one season (the record until broken by Maury Wills's 104 in 1962 and then Lou Brock's 118 in 1974).

Many years later, in the 1960s, a youngster asked Lefty O'Doul what he thought Cobb would hit now, against today's pitchers. "Oh, about .340, something like that," O'Doul replied.

It is 1909 and the Detroit Tigers are in the thick of the pennant race. Outfielder Sam Crawford is behind the wheel, second baseman Germany Schaefer beside him, and shortstop Donie Bush in the back seat.

Deacon Phillippe.

Sam Leever.

Star Pittsburgh Pitchers in the Early 1900s.

"Then why do you say Cobb was so great," the youngster asked, "if he could only hit .340 or so with this lively ball?"

"Well," O'Doul answered, "you have to take into consideration the man would now be seventy-eight years old!"

But statistics, no matter how awe-inspiring, give only a faint idea of the way Cobb dominated the playing field for over two decades. He could break open a close game single-handed. Not with one Ruthian swing of the bat, which took just a second, but with dramatic orchestration that extended over an interminable period of time. A perfectly placed bunt for a single ... inching farther and farther off first base to distract the pitcher ... as the pitcher goes into his delivery, a sudden dash toward second base ... a wild throw by the jittery catcher, with Cobb taking third on the throw ... and then, amid mounting tension, the final climax ... a false start ... another false start ... and suddenly a blur on the base path, a cloud of dust, and a spikes-high slide over home plate. He successfully stole home 35 times in his career! When

George Gibson, Pittsburgh catcher from 1905 through 1916 and then the Pirates' manager in the twenties and thirties.

Left to right: Pittsburgh Pirates' manager and left fielder Fred Clarke, center fielder Tommy Leach, and shortstop Honus Wagner, circa 1907.

Cobb stepped into the batter's box in the late innings of a close game, the crowd stirred audibly and edged forward—with excited anticipation at home in Detroit, with nervous apprehension in the seven other cities around the league.

Not only was Cobb the greatest player of his generation, perhaps of all time, but he was also the most disliked player of his generation, perhaps of all time. On the field, John McGraw and Ty Cobb were similar in many respects, but as a human being McGraw had admirable traits that at least partly offset his less commendable ones, while Cobb seemed to have few virtues if any. He is a perfect illustration of the proposition that greatness and goodness are separable—some would say incompatible—qualities. From all the evidence, Cobb was mean, selfish, bigoted, arrogant, and cold as ice. His drive to excel, to win, to be number one, verged on the psychotic, leaving no room for kindness, compassion, or friendship. Neither his teammates nor his family could get along with him, and as time went on he had fewer and fewer friends, in baseball or out. When he died in 1961, only three men from all of major league baseball attended his funeral.

The ingredients that created such a domineering personality will never be known, but one little-discussed incident had to leave a lasting impression. When he was eighteen years old his mother shot and killed his father, whom Ty worshiped. The senior Cobb tried to set a trap for his wife, suspecting her of infidelity. He told her he would be away for a few days and then returned home late at night, climbing through a window. His frightened wife, Ty's mother, shot the intruder as he tried to quietly climb over the windowsill in the dark. It can be only conjecture, but in all likelihood the shock of that traumatic experience left deep and permanent scars.

Cobb was not, of course, the whole Detroit Tigers team in those pennant-winning years of 1907, 1908, and 1909. With him in the outfield were the effervescent Davy Jones in left and long-ball hitting Wahoo Sam Crawford (from Wahoo, Nebraska) in center field. Like Tinker and Evers, Cobb and Crawford had little affection for each other and rarely spoke. Hughie Jennings, a teammate of John McGraw's on the old Baltimore Orioles, was the Detroit manager. He spent a disproportionate amount of his time mediating disputes between Cobb and his teammates, Cobb and the umpires, and Cobb and the public at large.

Great as the Georgia Peach was, the Chicago Cubs still had the better team, and to make up for their humiliation the previous year at the hands of the Hitless Wonders they defeated the Tigers in the World Series two years in a row. Behind the strong pitching of

Honus Wagner (about 1909).

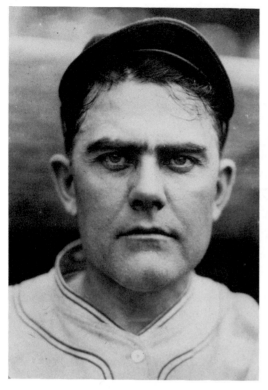

Babe Adams, winner of three complete games
in the 1909 World Series.

Wee Willie Keeler, hitting 'em where they ain't.

Three-Fingered Brown, Orvie Overall, Ed Reulbach, and Jack
Pfiester, the Cubs won the 1907 World Series four games to none,
and the 1908 Series four games to one.

In 1908, however, the World Series was anticlimactic, for it
was preceded by the famous Merkle incident and a resulting play-
off game between John McGraw's Giants and Frank Chance's Cubs
for the National League pennant. The play-off game created such a
fever pitch of excitement that the ensuing World Series could only
be a letdown.

Fred Merkle's boner, as it has come to be known, occurred in a
Cubs-Giants game at New York's Polo Grounds on September 23,
1908. In the bottom of the ninth, with the score tied 1-1 and two
out, the nineteen-year-old Merkle singled, advancing a teammate to

third and putting himself on first base. The next batter, Giant shortstop Al Bridwell, followed with a sharp single to center field. Merkle, seeing the man on third cross the plate with the apparent winning run, assumed the game was over—so instead of continuing all the way to touch second base he turned and ran for the clubhouse, to avoid the jubilant crowd surging onto the field.

But Johnny Evers, the quick-thinking Cub second baseman, shouted to center fielder Solly Hofman to throw him the ball. What happened thereafter is not clear, but evidently Hofman threw the ball in to Evers at second. The Giants' Iron Man Joe McGinnity, however, realizing what was about to happen, rushed on to the field, got to the ball ahead of Evers, and threw it as far as he could into the stands. Evers, not to be outmaneuvered, got another ball from somewhere, touched second base, and ran to the umpires screaming that Merkle was out, the inning was over, and the run didn't count.

After much confusion—pandemonium would be a better word—it was finally ruled that Johnny Evers was right. Since the crowd was all over the field by now, and it was getting dark anyway, the game was declared a 1-1 tie.

As fate would have it, the Giants and Cubs ended the season tied for first place, so the September 23 game had to be replayed as a special play-off game on October 8. The Cubs won, 4-2, with Frank Chance getting three hits and Three-Fingered Brown once again beating Matty.

For the rest of his days Fred Merkle would be blamed for losing the pennant in 1908. But actually Merkle shouldn't be blamed as much as Johnny Evers should be praised. For in those days it was commonplace for a base runner to dash for the clubhouse and neglect to touch second base on such a play. True, the rules are clear: when the third out of an inning is a force out at any base, a run cannot score on that play. But that particular rule had not been enforced on game-winning hits in the bottom of the ninth inning, with the game clearly ended, so Merkle was doing exactly as innumerable others had done before him. However, just a few weeks earlier the identical play had taken place against the Cubs, and Evers, who read the rule book instead of the backs of cereal boxes when he ate breakfast, had protested vigorously to the umpires. They remembered that protest and enforced the rule the next time it was called to their attention—again by Johnny Evers.

It is also unreasonable to blame Fred Merkle for losing the pennant when the Giants dropped a number of games **after** the Merkle boner. Two days later they lost both ends of a doubleheader to Cincinnati. And Harry Coveleski, a rookie pitcher for

Napoleon "Larry" Lajoie, the best second baseman in baseball in the early years of the century, many would say of all time. He hit .422 in 1901, .339 lifetime over a 21-year career.

LAJOIE
CHEWS
RED DEVIL
TOBACCO

Ask him if he don't

QUEEN CITY TOBACCO CO.
Cincinnati, O.

Two 1906 advertisements.

Lajoie says—
"I drink Coca-Cola regularly and have been doing so for several years. It is the most refreshing beverage an athlete can drink, and after a hard game I make my way to a Soda Fountain and get a glass. I can make $10,000 a year playing baseball, while I couldn't make more than 50 cents a day at anything else, and I am taking care of myself so that I may be in the game for several years yet to come."

A glass for you will cure that headache, run down and exhausted feeling. Brightens you up, refreshes and exhilerates you. Step into the first Soda Fountain and prove it for yourself.

Coca-Cola

is the best beverage for quenching the thirst. Refreshing and invigorating when one is in training and has none of the "let down" qualities of alcoholic beverages. A few bottles on the bench will quiet the nerves when the game is close

5c. Everywhere.

Waddell says—
More than once a bottle of your Coca-Cola has pulled me through a tight game. There is nothing better for pitchers in hot weather. I find Coca-Cola stimulating both to body and mind, and is the only beverage of the kind that does not leave an after effect. In every game I work, I keep a bottle or two on the bench for an emergency, and I can say that Coca-Cola has never yet failed me.
(Signed) G. E. (Rube) Waddell.

33

Philadelphia, earned the name of Giant Killer by beating them **three** times in the closing week of the season. Had the Giants won any of those games they would have ended the season in undisputed possession of first place.

John McGraw, the toughest taskmaster of all, never blamed Merkle for losing the pennant: Fred was the Giants' regular first baseman for the next eight years.

Poor Fred Merkle! If he had never gotten that hit to begin with, but had struck out, the inning would have been over and no one would have given him a second thought. But he singled, reached first base, and thereby set the stage for his own downfall. Forever after, whenever he got on first base, he would hear the same old refrain from the stands: "Hey Fred, don't forget to touch second."

The next year, 1909, neither the Cubs nor the Giants won the pennant. The Detroit Tigers won their third straight flag in the American League, but it was the Pittsburgh Pirates for a change in the National League, bringing Pirate shortstop Honus Wagner into a head-to-head confrontation with Ty Cobb in the World Series.

Those who saw them all are divided as to whether Ty Cobb, Babe Ruth, or Honus Wagner is the greatest baseball player who ever lived. John Peter Wagner could play any position on the diamond, although he finally settled at shortstop where for fifteen years he was the best in the game. Close to 6 feet tall and a solid 200 pounds, built like a weight lifter, as bow-legged as a pair of parentheses, Honus gobbled up anything hit in his vicinity, usually with a handful of dirt along with the ball, and fired the whole thing over to first base, dirt and all, in an awkward and yet somehow graceful motion.

Wagner hit .300 or better for 17 consecutive seasons, led the National League in batting eight times, and stole over 700 bases during his career. In temperament and personality he was the opposite of Cobb: modest to a fault, generous, sociable, and cuddly as a Teddy bear, all 200 pounds of him. He was popular with teammates and opponents alike, and loved by fans not only in Pittsburgh but in every city around the league.

As an aside, it might be noted that in 1908 Honus Wagner's salary was $5,000 a year, Ty Cobb's $4,500.

In later years Wagner recalled that the game was much rougher in those days. Veterans were jealous of their jobs and their status and didn't take kindly to rookies. He was in the league for three years, he remembered, before a star on an opposing team deigned to speak to him. Then, when Honus complimented him on a good play, the veteran snarled back: "Go to hell!"

"That made me very happy," Honus recalled, "at least he talked to me."

One story Honus loved to tell time and again was about Jimmy St. Vrain, a pitcher for the Chicago Cubs. Jimmy, who normally batted right-handed, was a terrible hitter. To see if he might possibly do better from the other side of the plate, Jimmy tried batting left-handed one day in a game against the Pirates. On the first pitch, St. Vrain tapped a slow roller to Wagner at shortstop and took off as fast he could go—but he was turned around and on the opposite side of the plate from where he was used to being and instead of running to first base he took off for **third!** Everyone in the ball park watched in astonishment as Jimmy raced to third base, head down, spikes flying, determined to get there ahead of the throw. And Honus, after fielding the ball, wasn't sure what to do with it himself.

"I'm standing there with the ball in my hand," Wagner said, "looking at this guy running from home to third, and for an instant I swear I didn't know **where** to throw the damn thing. And when I finally did throw to first, I wasn't at all sure it was the right thing to do."

Pittsburgh won the 1909 Series in seven games, with Pirate rookie Babe Adams achieving sudden fame by pitching three complete games and winning them all. And Wagner vanquished Cobb even more convincingly in the only direct encounter they ever had: Honus batted .333 to Cobb's .231 and stole six bases to Ty's two. On one occasion, when Cobb reached first base, he edged off, ready to steal, and shouted down to Wagner, "Watch out, Krauthead, I'm coming down. I'll cut you to pieces." And down he came, spikes high, but Wagner was ready: he held his ground and tagged Cobb so vigorously that several of Ty's teeth were jarred loose.

As the decade drew to a close, a number of the game's greatest pioneers began to come to the end of the trail. Wee Willie Keeler, for one, not quite 5 feet 5 inches tall, who said the idea is to "hit 'em where they ain't," which he did successfully for over 16 big league seasons. His lifetime batting average was .345.

And Napoleon "Larry" Lajoie, one of the smoothest fielding and hardest hitting second basemen of all time—so popular early in the century that for some years the Cleveland team was called the Naps in his honor. His lifetime batting average, over a 21-year career, was .339.

Not to mention Denton True "Cy" Young, the winningest pitcher in history. From 1890 through 1911 he won 508 games, with ten 20-game seasons and five 30-game ones.

But new stars were already in the wings, eagerly waiting their turn: Eddie Collins, Tris Speaker, Grover Cleveland Alexander, and Walter Johnson, to name but a few.

Denton True "Cy" Young in 1902, when at the age of thirty-five he won over 30 games for the fifth time in his career. From 1890 through 1911 he won more than 500 games.

Jack Barry.

Home Run Baker.
Stuffy McInnis.

Eddie Collins.

The Philadelphia Athletics'
$100,000 Infield.

Adolescence
1910-1919

THE Tinker-Evers-Chance plus Steinfeldt infield of the Chicago Cubs was getting on in years. In 1910 they made it to the World Series for the last time. By then Joe Tinker was thirty years old, Johnny Evers twenty-nine, Frank Chance thirty-three, and Harry Steinfeldt thirty-four. They had won four National League championships in five years and two World Series. But the end was near. In the 1910 Series they faced the future and succumbed to it.

What they faced was Cornelius McGillicuddy's rosy-cheeked new infield: Frank "Home Run" Baker, aged twenty-four, at third base; Jack Barry, aged twenty-three, at shortstop; Eddie Collins, aged twenty-three, at second; and the veteran Harry Davis, thirty-seven, at first base. Stuffy McInnis, only twenty, was on the bench; the following year he replaced Davis at first and completed the quartet that soon came to be known as Connie's $100,000 infield. The dollar figure referred not to what he had paid to get them, which was miniscule, but to their estimated market value if he were willing to sell them—and at that time $100,000 was considered an absolutely stupendous sum of money. With Chief Bender winning one game and Jack Coombs three, the Philadelphia Athletics walked over the Cubs in the 1910 Series, four games to one, beginning a dynasty that was to win the American League pennant three more times in the next four years (in 1911, '13, and '14).

Three of Connie Mack's all-time stalwarts: **left to right**, first baseman Harry Davis, pitcher Jack Coombs, and pitcher Eddie Plank.

Pitcher Rube Marquard in 1912, the year he won 19 straight games for the New York Giants (still the record for consecutive victories in a season).

Rube Marquard warms up before an admiring audience.

Over in the National League, McGraw was keeping pace with Mack. Building from the ground up, he was also fashioning a winner. With Buck Herzog at third base, Art Fletcher at shortstop, Larry Doyle at second, and Fred Merkle at first, and outfielders Fred Snodgrass, Red Murray, George Burns, and Josh Devore, the Giants regained their preeminence by taking three league championships in a row—1911, '12, and '13. Mathewson was still a winning pitcher (26 victories in 1911, 23 in 1912, and 25 in 1913), assisted by young Rube Marquard, while behind the plate a soft-spoken Cahuilla Indian, John Tortes Meyers, from southern California by way of Dartmouth College, hit .332 in 1911, .358 in 1912, and .312 in 1913.

"Chief" Meyers.

John Tortes "Chief" Meyers, Matty's catcher from
1909 through 1915. The Chief hit .332 in 1911,
.358 in 1912, and .312 in 1913.

Christy Mathewson, about 1912.

And so it came to pass that the paths of Mr. McGraw and Mr. Mack crossed again in 1911, diverged briefly, and then crossed once more in 1913. But now, unlike 1905, Connie emerged on top as the Philadelphia Athletics won the 1911 World Series, four games to two, and the 1913 Series, four games to one.

It was in the 1911 Series that the A's third baseman Frank Baker became "Home Run" Baker. He hit one in the second game to beat Marquard and another in the third game to beat Matty. That might not sound like so much today, but in the era of the "dead ball" two home runs in two days, particularly in a World Series, was a remarkable feat indeed, and it warranted giving the man responsible a nickname that would forever celebrate his prowess.

According to Chief Meyers, the Giants' catcher, at least part of Baker's success was attributable to the fact that the Athletics were able to "read" the Giants' pitchers. "They're getting our signs from someplace," Meyers told McGraw. "That coach on third base, Harry Davis, is calling our pitches. When he yells 'It's all right,' it's always a fast ball."

"He must be getting them off you," McGraw said.

So Meyers told Mathewson and Marquard to pitch whatever

Red Murray.

George Burns.

Three of the Giants' outfielders during their
pennant-winning years of 1911, 1912, and 1913.

Josh Devore.

Jim Thorpe, a Sac and Fox from Oklahoma and probably the greatest all-around athlete who ever lived. Thorpe was an outfielder for the New York Giants and the Cincinnati Reds from 1913 through 1919. He was also, at one time or another, an All-American college halfback, winner of the pentathlon and decathlon in the 1912 Olympics, and an outstanding professional football player. At the Olympics King Gustav V of Sweden told him, "You, sir, are the greatest athlete in the world." To which Jim Thorpe replied, "Thanks, King."

they wanted, and he'd catch them without signs. "But Davis still kept hollering 'It's all right' for the fast ball," Meyers later reported. "He knew something and we were never able to figure out what it was."

Frank Baker was not a great home run hitter by modern criteria—he never hit more than 12 in a season and had less than 100 lifetime. But by the standards of his day he ranked with the best. He led the American League in home runs four years in a row, 1911 through 1914—with 9, 10, 12, and 8—and in the days of the dead ball 39 home runs in four seasons was consistent power hitting.

After all, the offensive emphasis at that time was on place hitting, on spraying the ball around the diamond for singles and doubles, on precision bunting, the hit-and-run, and the stolen base. Ty Cobb, Wee Willie Keeler, and Honus Wagner honed such skills to perfection. And the 1911 New York Giants stole 347 bases, which is still the major league record. But their loss of the World Series because of Baker's home runs was a harbinger of things to come in the not-too-distant future.

Good as he was, Home Run Baker was not the brightest star in that Philadelphia infield. For at second base was Edward Trowbridge Collins, who many consider the best second baseman in all baseball history. His only rivals for that honor are Larry Lajoie, whose best years were behind him when Collins broke in; and Rogers Hornsby, Frank Frisch, Charlie Gehringer, Jackie Robinson, and Rod Carew, all of whom had yet to arrive on the scene.

Eddie Collins, aggressive, cocky, somewhat aloof, was an outstanding fielder, possibly not quite as graceful as Lajoie but equally effective. He was also a good enough hitter to compile a .333 lifetime batting average over a twenty-five-year major league career, and a good enough base runner—with 743 lifetime stolen bases—to rank third on the all-time list, right behind Lou Brock and Tyrus Raymond Cobb. (Opponents often complained that Collins had an unfair advantage that enabled him to steal so many bases; they claimed his jug-handle ears acted like sails, catching the wind and propelling him with extra speed along the base paths.) But, above all, Eddie Collins was the smartest kid on the block, his mind always working in high gear, always thinking, like a chess champion, several moves ahead. A Columbia University graduate, Collins was Connie Mack's all-time favorite and his heir apparent as manager of the Athletics—except that Connie didn't retire until 1950, when he was eighty-eight years old, and by then Eddie himself was in his sixties

The famous Boston Red Sox outfield during the years 1910-15.

Duffy Lewis.

Harry Hooper.

Tris Speaker.

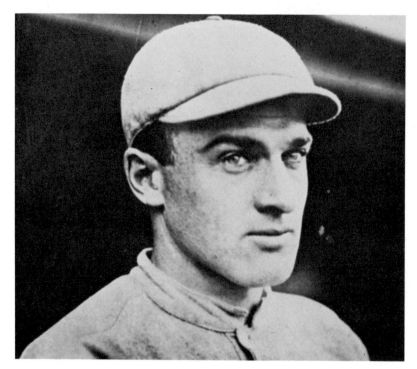

Third baseman Larry Gardner hit .315 for Boston in 1912. He played
with the Red Sox for ten years and with Cleveland for six.

Pitchers Smoky Joe Wood, **left,** and Christy Mathewson before the
start of the 1912 World Series. Smoky Joe won 34 games for the Red
Sox that season, and then three more in the World Series.

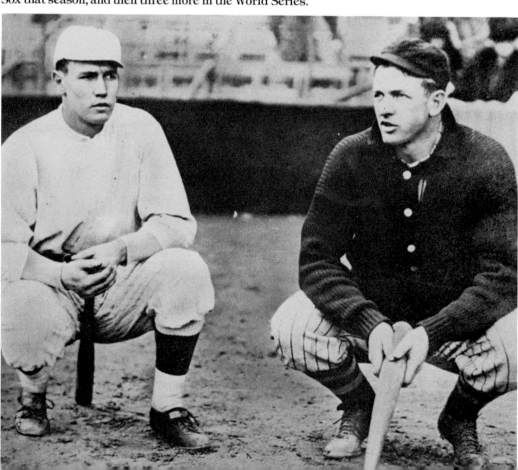

One of the games of the 1912 World Series, at Boston's brand-new Fenway Park.

Fred Snodgrass.

Although the Philadelphia Athletics won the American League flag in 1910 and 1911, and in 1913 and 1914, in 1912 the Boston Red Sox slipped in to take the pennant and the right to meet John McGraw's Giants in what turned out to be one of the most memorable of all World Series. The Red Sox boasted the meteoric Smoky Joe Wood on the mound (34 wins and 5 losses in 1912) and a defensive outfield that with the passage of time has acquired mythic proportions: Harry Hooper in right field, Duffy Lewis in left, and the incomparable Tris Speaker in center.

Speaker, a Texan with ruddy complexion and prematurely gray hair, had a .344 lifetime batting average over 21 seasons, with 3,515 hits—including 793 doubles, more than anyone else has ever hit. Nevertheless, he was even more renowned for his defensive abilities, hard as that may be to believe. The Gray Eagle played an extremely shallow center field, virtually a fifth infielder,

Dick Rudolph.

Bill James.

The pitching staff of the
1914 Miracle Braves. Dick
Rudolph won 27 games that
year, Bill James 26, and
Lefty Tyler 16. Then
Rudolph and James each
proceeded to win two games
from Connie Mack's
Athletics in the 1914 World
Series.

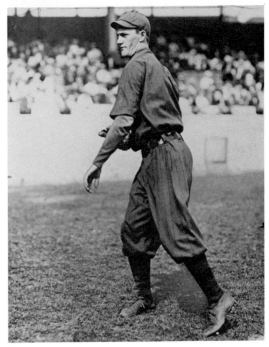

Lefty Tyler.

so that he often threw out opposing base runners by catching line drives over the infield that everyone assumed were safe hits and then throwing to a base before the frantic base runner could get back. Occasionally he even made unassisted double plays—spearing a low line drive and racing to the base himself before the surprised base runner could return. Speaker could play such a short center field because he was able to go back as fast as he could come in; he always claimed the few balls that got over his head for triples were far less damaging than the many potential singles he turned into outs by playing so close to the infield.

The Boston Red Sox won the 1912 Series, four games to three, with the deciding game, on October 16, going down to the proverbial wire. At the end of nine innings the score was tied, 1-1.

Grover Cleveland Alexander.

Lou Criger, for 15 years a catcher in the big leagues (from 1896 through 1910). Cy Young often said that Lou was the best catcher he had ever worked with.

Grover Cleveland Alexander in 1915, the year he won 31 games. In 1916 he won 33, with 16 shutouts.

In the top of the tenth, Giant outfielder Red Murray doubled off Joe Wood, and scored a moment later on a single by Fred Merkle. Thus the score was 2-1 in the Giants' favor going into the bottom of the tenth, and with Matty on the mound it looked as though the Giants were about to win their first Series since 1905.

But John McGraw was born under two stars, a lucky and an unlucky one, and the latter always seemed to take over at the most unexpected times. First the Merkle boner, and now Fred Snodgrass's equally notorious "$30,000 muff"!

Clyde Engle, first up for Boston in the bottom of the tenth inning, lofted a high fly to Fred Snodgrass in center field. Snodgrass settled under it, waited for it to come down, and then **dropped** it. Harry Hooper followed with a long drive to deep center; it had "double" written all over it, but this one Snodgrass hauled in over his shoulder after a long run. However, Mathewson, unsettled, walked the next batter, Boston second baseman Steve Yerkes, bringing Tris Speaker to the plate. The Gray Eagle popped up in foul territory midway between home plate and first base; first baseman Fred Merkle, catcher Chief Meyers, or Mathewson all could have caught it, but each evidently expected the other to—and so no one did! Given a new life, Speaker singled to right field, scoring Engle (the man Snodgrass had put on) with the tying run, and sending Yerkes (the man Mathewson had walked) to third base. A long fly by Boston third baseman Larry Gardner then scored Yerkes with the winning run, and the World Series was over.

Thus Fred Snodgrass's "$30,000 muff" (the dollar amount was the difference between the winning and losing team's share of the Series money) entered the Annals of the National Pastime, never to be forgotten. All that most people vaguely know is that "Snodgrass once dropped a fly ball and lost a World Series for the Giants."

But was Fred Snodgrass really responsible for the Giants losing the 1912 World Series? Not quite. He helped, of course, by putting the tying run on base. But he only put it on second base, not across home plate, and he had nothing at all to do with the winning run. Matty's loss of control (he put the winning run on base with a walk) and Matty, Merkle, and Meyers giving Speaker another chance (by letting his foul pop-up fall untouched) have to bear part of the responsibility for the loss.

Snodgrass made his error in 1912, when he was twenty-four years old. But, like Merkle, and Ralph Branca, as yet unborn, he had to live with it forever. Sixty-two years later, when he died in 1974, his obituary in the **New York Times** was headlined: "Fred, Snodgrass, 86, Dead; Ballplayer Muffed 1912 Fly."

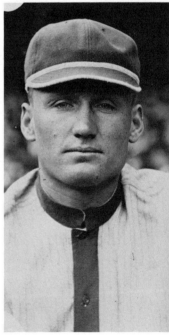

Four photos of Walter Johnson. (**Above**, with teammate Clyde Milan.)

Three .400 hitters, **left to right:** Shoeless Joe Jackson, Ty Cobb, and Larry Lajoie. This picture was taken in 1912. (Jackson hit .408 in 1911; Lajoie hit .422 in 1901; and Ty Cobb hit over .400 three times—.420 in 1911, .410 in 1912, and .401 in 1922.)

Just to make the record more complete: Fred Snodgrass joined the Giants in 1908, at the age of twenty, never having played a day in the minors; he was in the big leagues for nine years; in 1910 he batted .321; his lifetime batting average was .275; and he stole over 200 bases. He was a good ballplayer, who had the misfortune to make an error at the wrong time. John McGraw understood: his reaction to the dropped ball was to give Snodgrass a substantial salary increase for the following season.

In 1914 Connie Mack's Philadelphia Athletics won the American League pennant for the fourth time in five years. With Chief Bender, Eddie Plank, Home Run Baker, Eddie Collins, and other veteran stars, they were overwhelming favorites to win the World Series against the Boston Braves. Boston's Miracle Braves, they were called, because they rose from last place in the league standings on July 19 to first place by the end of the season. The

Gavvy Cravath in 1915, the year he hit a record 24 home runs for the Phillies. (It was Cravath's post-1900 record that Babe Ruth broke when he hit 29 in 1919.)

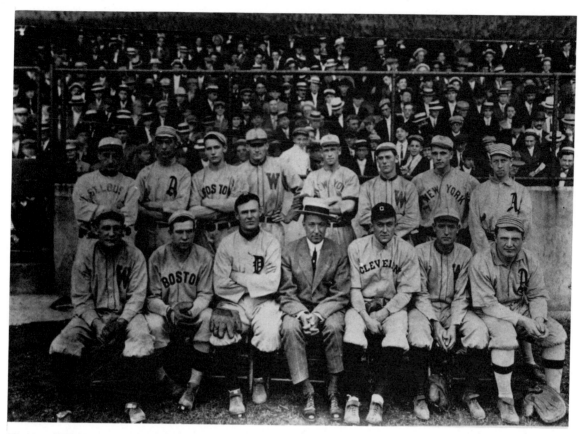

The first All-Star team (1911). After Cleveland pitcher Addie Joss died in the spring of 1911, an American League All-Star team, **above**, was organized to play a special exhibition game against Cleveland for the benefit of Addie Joss's widow. (The All-Stars won, 7-2.)

Front row, left to right: Germany Schaefer (2B), Tris Speaker (CF), Sam Crawford (RF), Jimmy McAleer (Mgr.), Ty Cobb, in borrowed uniform (LF), Gabby Street (C), and Paddy Livingston (C).

Back row, left to right: Bobby Wallace (SS), Home Run Baker (3B), Joe Wood (P), Walter Johnson (P), Hal Chase (1B), Clyde Milan (CF), Russell Ford (P), Eddie Collins (2B).

Heinie Zimmerman, infielder for the Chicago Cubs from 1907 to 1916, and then for the Giants until 1919. He batted .372 in 1912.

Zack Wheat.

Three Brooklyn Dodger heroes of an earlier era. Zack Wheat, Dodger outfielder from 1909 through 1926, had a .317 lifetime batting average. Nap Rucker won 22 games for Brooklyn in 1911, 18 the following year. Jeff Pfeffer won 23 games in 1914, 25 in 1916.

Nap Rucker.

Jeff Pfeffer.

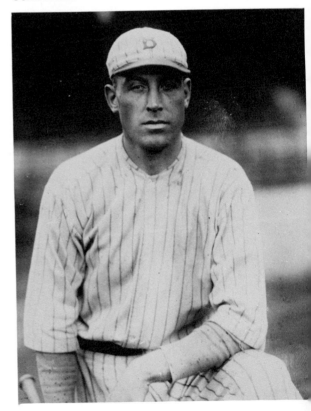

Miracle Braves continued to play inspired baseball in the Series, taking the measure of the mighty Philadelphia Athletics in four straight games—an upset so stunning it ranks with the victory of the Hitless Wonders over Frank Chance's Cubs in 1906 and sinking of the Spanish Armada by the English in 1588. That winter a disgruntled Connie Mack dismantled his great team, selling off his stars; he wouldn't have another winner until 1929.

The following year, 1915, it was again a Boston-Philadelphia World Series, but this time the contestants were the Boston Red Sox and, for the first time, the Philadelphia Phillies. The Phillies had a less glorious past than the Red Sox, and a less promising future as well—they wouldn't win another pennant until 1950. But they had one asset that was worth its weight in gold: pitcher Grover Cleveland Alexander.

Wilbur Cooper pitched for the Pittsburgh Pirates from 1912 through 1924. He won 20 or more games four times, 216 lifetime.

Grover Cleveland Alexander, Walter Perry Johnson, and Christopher Mathewson—unquestionably the three greatest pitchers of baseball's first quarter century, and many would say of all time. Alexander arrived in the big leagues in 1911, a shy, gangling, freckle-faced, sandy-haired youngster from Nebraska. He won 28 games his first season, and in 1915, '16, and '17 he won 31, 33, and 30 games respectively, duplicating Mathewson's great years 1903, '04, and '05. It was not easy to score runs off Alexander: he had 16 shutouts in one season, a record that still stands, 90 shutouts over his long career of 20 years. The only pitcher who ever hurled more shutouts was Walter Johnson, with 113 over 21 seasons.

Alexander's feats are all the more astonishing when one realizes he accomplished so many of them while pitching for the Phillies, whose home field—Baker Bowl—was a well-known hitter's paradise, with a right field wall so close that first basemen going back for a short pop fly had to be careful they didn't bump into the right fielder. Even so, Alex won 190 games in his seven years with the Phillies and another 183 with the Cubs and the Cardinals, for a grand total of 373—tied with Christy Mathewson for third place in the all-time rankings. Only two pitchers have ever won more games, Cy Young (508) and Walter Johnson (416).

Despite his success on the field, however, the lanky Nebraskan could never exorcise the personal demons that haunted him throughout his life and especially after he returned from the front lines in World War I. He suffered from epilepsy and from time to time had seizures in the dugout, although never while on the pitching mound. He became an alcoholic as well, less and less able to control his addiction with the passage of time. The final years of his life were racked with pain and suffering, poverty and delirium tremens, until at last he found peace on November 4, 1950.

While Alex was pitching shutouts in the National League, Walter Perry Johnson was doing the same in the American League. Walter was born in Humboldt, Kansas, in 1887, and as a teen-ager played semipro ball in the Northwest for a couple of years before joining the Washington Senators at the age of nineteen. Thereafter, he never wore the uniform of another team during his playing career, which lasted for 21 years.

Walter was a tall, slim, easygoing man, with unusually long arms that whipped the ball over the plate as though it were hurled by a slingshot. His main pitch, for years virtually his only pitch, was his famed fastball. Like Bob Feller's a generation later, and Nolan Ryan's after that, batters often saw only a blur. Indeed, Johnson's greatest fear was that he might injure a batter; some, like

George "Hooks" Dauss, outstanding Detroit right-hander from 1912 through 1926. He won over 20 games three times, 221 lifetime.

George Herman Ruth, Boston Red Sox pitcher, in 1916. He won 23 games that year, 24 the following year.

Fred Toney.

The date was May 2, 1917, when Fred Toney of Cincinnati and Hippo Vaughn of the Cubs **both** pitched no-hitters through nine innings. Toney won in the tenth when Vaughn allowed two hits and the game's only run.

Jim "Hippo" Vaughn.

Bullet Joe Bush in 1916, when he won 15 games for Connie Mack's Athletics. Later, he won 26 games for the Yankees in 1922.

Third baseman Heinie Groh
and his famous bottle bat.

← Babe Ruth in 1918. By this
time people were starting to
think of him for his hitting
as much as for his pitching.
In 1918 he won 13 games as
a pitcher and at the same
time tied for the league lead
in home runs (with 11).

Cobb, took advantage of his gentle nature by deliberately crowding
the plate, knowing he would slow down a bit rather than hurt
anyone.

Washington outfielder Clyde Milan roomed with Johnson for
14 years. "He not only had the greatest arm of all time but the finest
disposition you could imagine," Milan said years later. "He had
some sort of phobia about young fellows breaking into baseball.
He'd never embarrass them. If we had a comfortable lead, he'd
always lay in nice fat ones for rookies and let them hit it. Once a
youngster got four hits off Walter, and when the fellow came up for
the fifth time, Walter didn't try to get even. Just the opposite—he
tossed the ball up to him nice and easy, so the kid could get five for
five. When the youngster popped up, I think Walter was more
disappointed than the batter."

Johnson rarely pitched with a good ball club behind him. In his first 17 seasons with Washington, only six times did the team win more games than it lost. Thus Walter didn't get to play in a World Series until 1924, when his career was almost at an end. Nevertheless, he is the all-time leader in strikeouts (3,508) and shutouts (113), and in games won (416) he is second only to Cy Young's unapproachable total of 508. Actually, Walter Johnson did win more games than any other pitcher in the twentieth century, since Cy Young won 265 of his 508 victories before 1900.

The Boston Red Sox defeated the Philadelphia Phillies in the 1915 World Series, despite the presence of Alexander and Gavvy Cravath, six-time National League home run leader. Cravath hit 24 homers for the Phillies that year to set a record that everyone thought would last for years.

The Red Sox followed up their 1915 World Series victory by defeating the Brooklyn Dodgers in 1916 and the Chicago Cubs in 1918. Three World Championships in four years, matching the record of Connie Mack's Athletics in the years 1910 through 1913! The Red Sox were a very good team, potentially a great one, with particularly strong pitching: Carl Mays, Sad Sam Jones, Bullet Joe Bush, Herb Pennock, and a blithe-spirited young left-hander who had come to the Red Sox in 1914 at the age of nineteen. He proceeded to win 23 games in 1916, 24 in 1917, and pitched 29 consecutive scoreless World Series innings in 1916 and 1918. His name was George Herman Ruth, everyone called him Babe, and he appeared to have a promising future.

However, the potential Boston Red Sox dynasty was aborted when owner Harry Frazee started selling his players for cash in order to keep his theatrical ventures afloat. Within a few years practically the entire pitching staff—including George Herman Ruth, who by then had been turned into an outfielder—had been sold to the New York Yankees, along with a few others, and what should have been a Red Sox dynasty turned instead into a Yankee juggernaut.

Another potentially great team had also been built in the American League at about the same time: the Chicago White Sox, pennant winners in 1917 and 1919 and World Series winners in 1917. The White Sox had a fine infield, good catching, pitching as good as Boston's, and in the outfield one of the best hitters who ever lived—Shoeless Joe Jackson. Joseph Jefferson Jackson, of Brandon Mills, South Carolina, couldn't read or write, but he certainly could hit, as attested to by his .356 lifetime batting average—third highest in history, right behind Ty Cobb's .367 and Rogers Hornsby's .358. Jackson hit over .370 four times, once over

Edd Roush, popular center fielder for the Cincinnati Reds from 1916 through 1926 and for the New York Giants for several years thereafter. Roush batted over .350 in 1921, '22, and '23, and then in 1924 he slumped all the way to .348.

Utility infielder Fred McMullin.

The Chicago Black Sox.

Pitchers Lefty Williams and Eddie Cicotte.

Third baseman Buck Weaver.

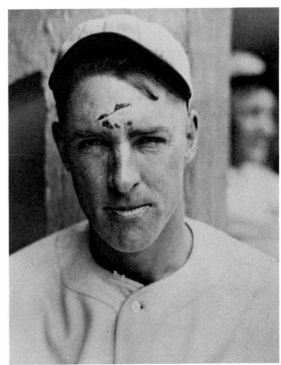

Shortstop Swede Risberg.

Outfielder Happy Felsch.

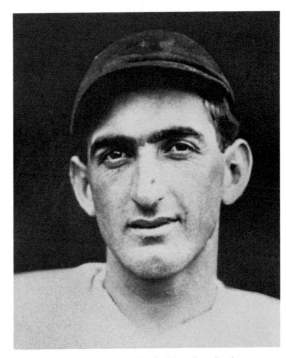

Outfielder Joe Jackson.

First baseman Chick Gandil.

.400, but never won a batting title because Ty Cobb or George Sisler always ended up just a bit higher.

Joe Jackson's illiteracy was widely known and a frequent subject for laughter. People chuckled at various versions of the widely repeated story that in restaurants he would always wait for another ballplayer to order first, since he couldn't read the menu, and then say "I'll have what he's having."

Shoeless Joe knew people made fun of him, and he didn't like it. Once he hit a long triple and, as he stood on third base, someone in the crowd raised snickers by shouting, "Hey Joe, can you spell 'cat'?" Joseph Jefferson Jackson looked over, squirted a stream of tobacco juice in the heckler's direction, and yelled back, "How about you, big shot—can you spell 'shit'?"

The Chicago White Sox were heavy favorites to win the World Series in 1919, just as they had won it two years earlier. The Cincinnati Reds, National League pennant winners, were a good team, led by center fielder Edd Roush and third baseman Heinie Groh, but on paper the Reds seemed to be no match for the powerful White Sox.

However, in an upset reminiscent of the 1914 Miracle Braves and the 1906 Hitless Wonders, the Reds trounced the White Sox, five games to three. (From 1919 through 1921 the World Series was extended to a five out of nine basis instead of the usual four out of seven.) There were ugly rumors that everything was not as it appeared to be, but such talk was typically dismissed as irresponsible if not downright unpatriotic.

Almost a year later the story broke: eight of the White Sox (thereafter to be known as the Black Sox) had been bribed by gamblers to lose the Series. Those implicated were first baseman Chick Gandil (evidently the ringleader), pitchers Eddie Cicotte and Lefty Williams, outfielder Happy Felsch, shortstop Swede Risberg, utility infielder Fred McMullin, and third baseman Buck Weaver, who knew about the fix but may or may not have participated in it.

And, yes, Shoeless Joe Jackson. As Shoeless Joe was leaving the courthouse in Chicago after confessing his involvement, a small boy, tears in his eyes, is reported to have tugged at his sleeve. "Say it ain't so, Joe," he pleaded.

Apocryphal or not, it was an entire nation that was praying it wasn't so. When it turned out to be all too true, the shock rocked the country. All those involved were banished from baseball for life. But a disillusioned public wondered about the extent of the corruption: if a World Series could be fixed, how many other games were being thrown? With confidence in the integrity of the game shattered, baseball itself was on trial.

Little Dickie Kerr, 5 feet 7 inches tall and 155 pounds, was one of the White Sox the fixers did **not** get to. He won two games in the 1919 Series.

Hal Chase, thought by many to be the best fielding first baseman of all time, was reportedly involved in fixing games even before the 1919 scandal.

George Herman Ruth.

It was saved by two men whose backgrounds and temperaments could not have been more disparate: a stern-visaged patrician federal judge from Indiana and an uninhibited pitcher-turned-outfielder only a few years out of a Baltimore reform school. Their names were Kenesaw Mountain Landis and George Herman Ruth.

The One and Only.

The One and Only
1920-1929

GEORGE HERMAN RUTH not only helped save baseball but also seemed to re-create it in his own image. With his sweeping, powerful, flawless swing, he immediately made obsolete all previous slugging records and set standards for distance hitting that still exist today. At the same time, he became the greatest hero in the history of American sports, a genuine American legend, the centerpiece of the madcap twenties when the country went on a decade-long binge of unprecedented proportions. All of it—the exuberance, the irresponsibility, the magical joy—seemed embodied in and represented by Babe Ruth.

With his moon face, skinny legs, and the considerable paunch he developed with the passage of time, he was a most unlikely-looking hero. He was a drinker, a womanizer, a glutton; he could be coarse, gross, arrogant, childishly rebellious. But at the same time there lay in this mammoth talent wellsprings of kindness and generosity that radiated out to his adoring public. The Babe had a special affection for children. He would stand for hours, tirelessly and patiently signing autographs. Once, upon leaving a ball park (when most players are anxious to get home or back to their hotels), he found himself confronted by a huge crowd of autograph seekers. Ruth promptly asked an attendant to bring a chair, whereupon he sat himself down and remained there long after dark, until every fan had been satisfied.

Born on February 6, 1895, Ruth was the son of a Baltimore saloonkeeper. By all accounts (including his own) a difficult and unruly child, he was at the age of eight brought by his parents to St. Mary's Industrial School for Boys in Baltimore, an institution run by Xaverian Brothers. For most of the next decade St. Mary's was his home.

The institution had a highly developed baseball program, and young George Ruth soon became its star. Eventually word got around about the hard-hitting pitcher at St. Mary's, and in February of 1914, when he was nineteen, Ruth signed his first professional contract, for $100 a month.

The man who signed him was Jack Dunn, owner and manager of the Baltimore Orioles, then of the International League. Before the 1914 season was over Ruth was in the major leagues, pitching for the Boston Red Sox. Dunn had sold Ruth, pitcher Ernie Shore, and another player to the Red Sox for around $20,000. Jack Dunn's baby, they called him, and in time it was shortened to "Babe." John McGraw had been interested in Ruth but was never given the opportunity to bid for him, something for which McGraw never forgave Dunn. Baseball fans might enjoy speculating about the sparks that would have been ignited if the freewheeling Ruth and the authoritarian McGraw had ever been together on the same team.

Ruth's sale to pennant-hungry Yankee owner Jacob Ruppert on January 3, 1920, for approximately $125,000, was a landmark event in baseball history; it was, in effect, the beginning of the New York Yankee dynasty, a dynasty that was to produce 29 pennants in the next 45 years. Ruth was only part of the Red Sox migration to New York. Over the next few years he was followed by pitchers Waite Hoyt, Carl Mays, Joe Bush, Sam Jones, Herb Pennock, infielders Joe Dugan and Everett Scott, and catcher Wally Schang. By 1923 the rape of the Red Sox was complete. Boston's own modest dynasty was over. From 1922 through 1930 they finished dead last eight times.

In 1920 Ruth's long-distance hitting and magnetic personality raised baseball higher in the national consciousness than it had ever been. In his first year as a Yankee he wreaked devastation with his bat that had no parallel in baseball history. He hit .376, drove in 137 runs, scored 158, and hit an unbelievable 54 home runs. To underscore the phenomenon of that latter figure, one need only note that only one other team in the league, the St. Louis Browns, hit as many as 50 home runs.

That same watershed year, 1920, saw the installation of baseball's first, and greatest, commissioner. Kenesaw Mountain

A trim young Babe Ruth in 1922.

Babe Ruth and friends in 1922.

Kenesaw Mountain Landis.

Landis (he was named after a Civil War battle in Georgia) was the choice of the alarmed and panicky club owners to restore public faith in baseball's integrity after the scandal of the 1919 World Series. Appointed a federal judge by President Theodore Roosevelt in 1905, the fifty-four-year-old Landis demanded, and received, sweeping powers. He alone would decide who and what was to the game's benefit or detriment. His decisions were closed to appeal. Whenever the owners grew restive under Landis's autocratic rule, the judge offered to tear up his $50,000-a-year contract and resign. Invariably the owners backed down.

Landis's decisiveness—some said his ruthlessness—in his handling of the Black Sox scandal helped restore confidence in the game. Landis remained in office for almost a quarter of a century, until his death in 1944. By that time the white-haired judge had become an integral part of the game, and pictures of his frowning face, chin resting on his hands on the railing of his box seat at ball games, had become familiar to fans everywhere.

It was inevitable that Ruth, the great rule breaker, and Landis, the uncompromising rule maker, should clash. After the 1921 World Series, in which the Yankees participated, Ruth headed a barnstorming team that traveled around the country. This was in violation of a then-existing rule forbidding barnstorming by World Series participants. When Ruth heard that Landis meant to enforce the rule, the Babe said, "Tell the old guy to go jump in the lake," and blithely went ahead with his tour, along with teammate Bob Meusel.

Landis bided his time and, late in 1921, announced his decision—Ruth and Meusel were fined their full World Series shares ($3,500 apiece) and suspended for the first six weeks of the 1922 season. Landis's handling of the great Babe probably put more muscle into the commissioner's office than any other single act.

In spite of Ruth's heroics, however, the Yankees failed to win the pennant in 1920, finishing third, three games behind the Cleveland Indians. Until 1920 the American League pennant had been monopolized by four teams—Philadelphia, Boston, Detroit, and Chicago. Cleveland was the first of the "poor cousins" to break through. They did it on the strength of player-manager Tris Speaker's .388 batting average, Jim Bagby's 31 wins, and 20-plus seasons by spitballer Stanley Coveleski and Ray Caldwell. And they did it despite the most crushing tragedy ever to occur on a baseball field.

On August 16, 1920, at the Polo Grounds (at that time the home of the Yankees as well as the Giants), Yankee pitcher Carl Mays threw a high inside pitch that slammed into the head of Cleveland's fine shortstop, Ray Chapman. Chapman crumpled at the plate. He died the next day of a skull fracture. It remains the only fatality ever to occur on a major league ball field. Adding irony to the tragedy is the fact that the twenty-nine-year-old Chapman was said to have been considering retirement from the game after the season.

Speaker was able to rally his demoralized team, and with the aid of rookie Joe Sewell, called up from the minors to replace Chapman, the Indians went on to win the pennant. For Sewell, it was the beginning of a remarkable career that would ultimately end in the Hall of Fame.

As another indication that 1920 was bringing a changing of the guard, it was the end of Ty Cobb's remarkable string of 12 American League batting championships in 13 years. St. Louis' dazzling first baseman, George Sisler, won the batting title with a .407 average, driving out 257 hits in the process, a record that still

Jim Bagby. Bagby aston-
ished everyone by winning
31 games for Cleveland in
1920. His stay at the top
was brief; two years later he
won 4 and lost 5 and soon
left the big leagues. His son,
Jim Jr., pitched for Boston
and Cleveland in the
thirties and forties.

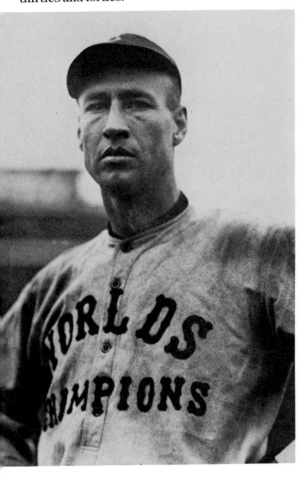

The pitching Coveleski brothers, Harry on
the left and Stanley on the right. Harry was
a three-time 20-game winner for the Tigers
from 1914 through 1916. Stanley, one of the
great spitballers of all time, won three
games for Cleveland in the 1920 World
Series and 214 over his career. They would
never pitch against each other, as a matter
of principle.

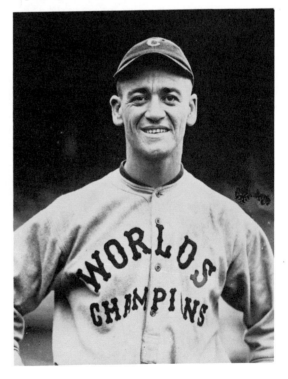

George Burns played first base in the American League
from 1914 through 1929. A lifetime .307 hitter, Burns
hit 64 doubles in 1926, the second-highest single-
season total in history. (Earl Webb had 67 for the Red
Sox in 1931; the Cardinals' Joe Medwick also had 64, in
1936.)

stands. The St. Louis Browns also featured an outfield of Jack Tobin, Baby Doll Jacobson, and Ken Williams, all of whom hit well over .300 during the early twenties.

The 1920 World Series pitted the Cleveland Indians against the Brooklyn Robins, so called after their colorful manager, Wilbert Robinson. The Series was notable for the occurrence of one of those bizarre happenings that invariably seemed to characterize a Brooklyn World Series.

In the fifth game of the Series, which Cleveland was to win five games to two (this was the second year of a three-year experiment with a nine-game Series), Bill Wambsganss, the Indians' second baseman, had baseball immortality virtually thrust upon him. Pete Kilduff and Otto Miller opened the top of the Brooklyn fifth with singles. Then Clarence Mitchell, the Brooklyn pitcher, hit a scorching line drive that Wambsganss brought down with an extraordinary leap. Thinking it a sure base hit, Kilduff and Miller were off with the crack of the bat. Wambsganss stepped on second to double up Kilduff and was about to throw to first when shortstop

This 1920 Cleveland double-play combination would have their names etched upon the scrolls of baseball history—tragically for shortstop Ray Chapman, **left**, gloriously for second baseman Bill Wambsganss, **right**.

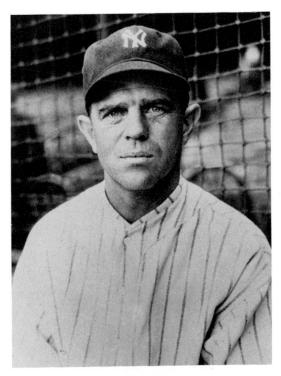

Joe Sewell. Called up from the minor leagues to replace the fallen Chapman, Sewell went on to a remarkable career. He was simply the most difficult man to strike out in baseball history. In 1925 he went to bat 672 times and fanned just four times. In 1932 he struck out just three times in 559 times at bat. He played in the major leagues 14 years and in that time struck out only 114 times in over 7,900 times at bat. Once, when asked by a teammate how he avoided striking out, Sewell explained: "It's very simple . . . you just keep your eye on the ball."

Elmer Smith hit the first grand-slam home run in World Series history, against Brooklyn in 1920.

Joe Sewell saw what Wambsganss did not—Miller had not stopped running. "Tag him! Tag him!" Sewell yelled. The startled Wambsganss looked around, found an even more startled Miller coming at him, applied the tag, and completed the only unassisted triple play in World Series history and one of the few in all of baseball history.

The crowd was stunned for a moment, and then, realizing what had happened, stood and cheered—many of the spectators throwing their hats out onto the field to show their appreciation.

On his next trip to the plate Clarence Mitchell set some sort of record for offensive frustration when he hit into a double play, thus accounting for five outs in two trips to the plate.

In 1921 the Yankees finally won their first pennant. It came on the strength of the pitching of Carl Mays, Waite Hoyt, and Bob Shawkey, and the hitting of Babe Ruth. The hitting was awesome, even by Ruth's standards. For the third consecutive year he set a home run record, his 59 homers eclipsing the 54 he had hit the year before and more than doubling the record 29 he had hit in 1919. Indeed, 1921 was Ruth's greatest season at the plate, perhaps the greatest any hitter has ever had. Along with his 59 home runs, he had 44 doubles and 16 triples, scored 177 runs, drove in 170, and batted .378!

Joe Oeschger of the Boston Braves. ·

Leon Cadore of the Brooklyn Robins.

For endurance and efficiency, no two pitchers have ever approached what these two right-handers did on May 1, 1920, at Braves Field in Boston. At the end of six innings the score was tied, 1-1. At the end of 26 innings, it was still 1-1 as darkness fell and the game was declared a tie. It was the longest game ever played in major league history, and Oeschger and Cadore both pitched the entire distance.

Ken Williams, an outstanding hitter for the St. Louis Browns in the 1920s. He led the American League with 39 home runs and 155 runs batted in in 1922.

George Sisler.

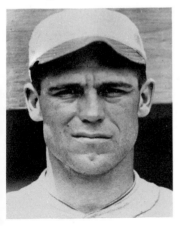

In the National League, John McGraw's Giants were champions again in 1921, thus creating what was to be the first of many all-New York World Series. It was also the first of an unprecedented four straight pennants for McGraw, and the first of three consecutive Yankee-Giant World Series. With the two teams still sharing the same ball park, the 1921 and 1922 World Series were played in their entirety at the Polo Grounds. The World Series of 1923 opened at the Yankees' brand-new ball park—Yankee Stadium, the largest and most majestic stadium built up to that time, and still a symbol of baseball grandeur.

After losing the 1921 and 1922 Series to the Giants, the Yankees finally won their first World Championship in 1923, despite some home run heroics for the Giants by a journeyman outfielder named Casey Stengel.

While Babe Ruth's performances on the field and his antics away from it were commanding the headlines throughout much of the 1920s, a young Texan playing second base for the St. Louis Cardinals had begun a decade of high-average hitting that is unlikely ever to be approached. Described by many of his contemporaries as possessing "the coldest eyes" they ever saw, Rogers Hornsby was a brutally frank and outspoken man. He was also the greatest right-handed hitter the game has ever known. Beginning in 1920, Hornsby led the National League in batting six consecutive times: his five-year batting average from 1921 through 1925 was over .400, and his average for the full decade was over .380. In 1922 St. Louis was the batting capital of the world, with George Sisler hitting .420 for the Browns and Hornsby .401 for the Cardinals, amassing 496 hits between them.

Hornsby's concentration on hitting had laser-beam qualities. Nothing else, it seemed, was allowed to enter his mind. He seldom read books or newspapers or went to the movies, for fear of weakening his eyes. The only thing that even remotely rivaled his interest in baseball was his penchant for betting on horse races. When asked why, unlike so many other ballplayers, he did not play golf, Hornsby snapped, "When I hit a ball, I want somebody else to chase it."

Years later, when he was managing Cincinnati in the early fifties, Hornsby's passion for hitting remained undiminished. One day, before a game with the Phillies, one of the Philadelphia players happened to ask Hornsby a question about batting during pregame practice. Hornsby picked up a bat to demonstrate his answer, and in a few minutes a half dozen Phillies were standing in a circle solemnly listening to the Cincinnati manager give them batting tips!

Urban Shocker. He won 20 games
or more for the St. Louis Browns
from 1920 through 1923, hitting
his peak in 1921 with 27 victories. On September 6, 1924, he
pitched two complete games of a
doubleheader and won them both.
Later, he starred on the mound
for the 1927 Yankees.

William Chester "Baby
Doll" Jacobson was part of
the Browns' powerful lineup
in the early 1920s. In 1920
and 1921 he posted batting
averages of .355 and .352.

←

George Sisler in 1917.
Considered by many the
greatest first baseman of all
time, Sisler twice hit better
than .400 and had a lifetime
batting average of .340.

McGraw's Giants in the early twenties were perhaps his best
ever. The 1924 aggregation featured five future Hall of Famers—
Frank Frisch, Ross Youngs, George Kelly, and a pair of youngsters
named Bill Terry and Fred Lindstrom. In addition, McGraw's
beautifully balanced team included Hack Wilson, Irish Meusel,
Travis Jackson, and Heinie Groh, who used an oddly shaped bat
that resembled a bottle.

The Giants were matched against the Washington Senators in
the 1924 World Series and it was an occasion for high drama. Not
only was it Washington's first World Series, but it was also the first
for the man who seemed to personify the Washington ball club—
the beloved Walter Johnson. Pitching in his eighteenth season,
Johnson still had enough on his fastball to win 23 games, lead the
league in earned run average, in strikeouts for the twelfth time, and
in shutouts for the seventh. The only thing that had been denied
Johnson in his illustrious career was a World Series victory. And
for a while it looked as though Walter was destined to be denied
forever.

Although the sentimental favorite Johnson pitched the opening game, the Giants won in 12 innings, 4-3. Walter also started and lost the fifth game, 6-2. Washington won the next day to even the Series at three games apiece, setting the stage for a memorable seventh game.

With the Giants leading, 3-1, in the bottom of the eighth inning of the seventh game, a bad-hop single with the bases loaded by Washington player-manager Bucky Harris tied the score. In the top of the ninth Walter Johnson emerged dramatically from the Washington bullpen. Johnson hurled four shutout innings in a deepening twilight. In the bottom of the twelfth Washington came to bat, the score still tied. A remarkable sequence of events followed.

With one out, Muddy Ruel lifted an easy pop foul behind the plate. As he tried to line up the ball, Giant catcher Hank Gowdy stepped on his own mask, losing both his footing and the ball. Thus reprieved, Ruel promptly doubled. Johnson came to bat with a storybook finish in sight—winning his own game. Instead, he grounded to shortstop Travis Jackson, who fumbled the ball, Ruel held second. Washington's Earl McNeely then hit a grounder toward third, possibly a double-play ball. But for the second time in the game Providence dropped a pebble in front of a Washington grounder and the ball bounced high over third baseman Fred Lindstrom's head and into left field, scoring the winning run. Walter Johnson had finally won a World Series game and a World Championship as well!

After the game, Giants' pitcher Jack Bentley, something of a clubhouse philosopher, had an explanation for the weird series of events: "The good Lord just couldn't bear to see a fine fellow like Walter Johnson lose again."

The 1926 World Series saw another legendary pitcher turn in an even more dramatic performance in the waning days of his career. Grover Cleveland Alexander was now thirty-nine years old, sickly, alcoholic, epileptic. Acquired on waivers in midseason from the Chicago Cubs, Alex helped pitch the St. Louis Cardinals to their first pennant, under player-manager Rogers Hornsby.

The Cardinals' opponents were the New York Yankees, back on top after a two-year absence. Ruth was still rocketing home runs, aided and abetted now by rookie Tony Lazzeri, Earle Combs, and a twenty-three-year-old youngster rounding out his second full season, Lou Gehrig.

The Series seesawed back and forth to a seventh game. Alexander had won the second and sixth games for the Cardinals, handling the hard-hitting Yankees with ease. The seventh game

John McGraw and Babe Ruth size each other up prior to the 1922 World Series between the Giants and the Yankees. The two never got along very well together, dating from McGraw's reported comment, when the Babe was still a pitcher, that "if he plays every day the bum will hit into a hundred double plays a season."

was played on a dreary, overcast October afternoon at Yankee Stadium. St. Louis starter Jesse Haines dueled Waite Hoyt to the bottom of the seventh inning, with the Cardinals ahead, 3-2. With two out and the bases loaded, Haines could no longer pitch because of blisters. Hornsby summoned Alex from the bullpen. Alexander had pitched nine innings the day before, and legend has it he had been out all night celebrating and was nursing a hangover in the bullpen. This is not true. When Alexander took the long, slow walk in to the pitching mound, he was cold sober and alert.

When he reached the mound, Alex told Hornsby how he planned to pitch the batter—rookie slugger Tony Lazzeri (also an epileptic).

"I'm giving him a fastball well inside on the first pitch," Alex said.

"You can't do that," Hornsby said. Lazzeri was a fastball hitter.

"Yes I can," Alex said. "If I get it far enough inside, he'll foul it. Then I have a strike on him. Then I'll give him curves on the outside that he won't touch."

Hornsby began to protest, then grinned.

"Who am I to tell **you** how to pitch?" the Cardinal manager said. "Go ahead. Do it your way."

Alex did it his way. Sure enough, Lazzeri jumped on the inside fastball and hit it hard and far, but clearly foul—a foul ball that is still reverberating through baseball history. Alex then struck him out on two sharp-breaking curve balls and shuffled off the mound, having notched what is to this day baseball's most famous strikeout.

He retired the Yankees in order in the eighth, got the first two men in the ninth, and then, pitching carefully, walked Ruth on a 3-2 pitch that Alex swore was strike three. When he got to first base, Ruth, unaccountably, tried to steal second. He was thrown out by a wide margin and the Cardinals were World Champions. Ruth's attempted steal was later described as "the only mistake the big monkey ever made on a ball field."

St. Louis fans were still basking in the glow of their first pennant and World Championship when they were stunned and outraged by the trading of their manager, chief slugger, and all-round hero, Rogers Hornsby. He was traded to the Giants for Frank Frisch and pitcher Jimmy Ring. The sharp-tongued Hornsby had made himself unpopular with owner Sam Breadon, and when he asked for a three-year contract at $50,000 per year, it was too much for the tight-fisted Breadon. Frisch, a dynamic, hustling player had made himself equally unpopular with McGraw—there was outright hatred between the two—and so the deal was made. Over the next

Yankee Stadium the day it opened, April 18, 1923.

Rogers Hornsby. Lifetime batting average: .358.

Ross Youngs was one of John McGraw's favorite players. A nonstop hustler, Youngs had a lifetime batting average of .322. He died in midcareer in 1927 at the age of thirty.

Jesse Barnes.

Two of John McGraw's top pitchers in the early twenties.

Art Nehf.

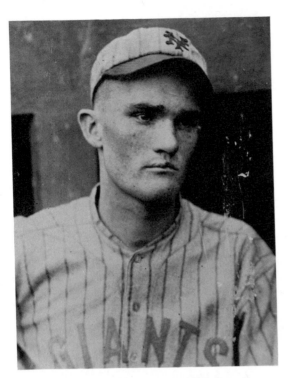

Red Lucas as a Giant rookie in 1923. Lucas was a winning pitcher with Cincinnati later in the decade. He was also one of the great hitting pitchers of all time. In 1929 and 1931 he led the National League in both complete games pitched and pinch hits.

Travis Jackson, one of the fine shortstops of his era, played his entire career with the New York Giants, from 1922 through 1936.

John McGraw standing on the batting cage to have a better look at Travis Jackson.

The Giants' Emil "Irish" Meusel in a familiar 1920s pose. Brother of the Yankees' Bob, Irish had a lifetime batting average of .310.

three years the abrasively outspoken Hornsby and his .380 batting average would play in New York, Boston, and Chicago, never able to accommodate to the world around him.

In 1927 Detroit's Harry Heilmann led the American League in batting for the fourth time. What made Heilmann's achievements unique was a strange consistency—he led the league only in odd-numbered years: 1921, '23, '25, and '27, with explosive batting averages of .394, .403, .393, and .398. It was rumored that two-year contracts, each ending in the odd-numbered years, accounted for Heilmann's surges. Nevertheless, in his "off" years, the line-driving-hitting Heilmann posted averages of .356, .346, and .367.

Frankie Frisch. One of the finest all-around ballplayers in history, the fiery Frisch and the dictatorial McGraw could not get along with each other. So in 1926, after eight scintillating years with the Giants, McGraw traded him to the Cardinals for Rogers Hornsby (with whom McGraw couldn't get along either).

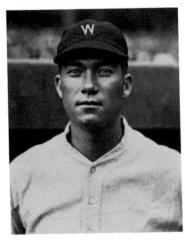

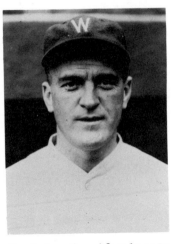

Fred Marberry of the Washington Senators, one of the earliest and best relief specialists.

Joe Judge played first base in the big leagues for 20 years, 18 of them with the Washington Senators (1915-32). He hit over .300 nine times.

Outfielder Sam Rice didn't get to the big leagues until he was twenty-five, but he played for 20 years anyway, 19 of them for Washington. A consistent .300 hitter, Rice finished with a .322 lifetime mark and an unusual total of 2,987 hits—unusual because he did not seem interested in those last 13.

Heilmann's four batting crowns, in addition to Cobb's 12 and one by Heinie Manush in 1926, gave Detroit 17 batting championships by 1927.

And then there were the Yankees—"The '27 Yankees"—a crisply descriptive phrase denoting what is generally regarded as the greatest team of all time. Their credentials are impressive. Ruth reached his home run peak that season with 60, hitting number 60 with typical Ruthian flair on his last at-bat of the season; young Lou Gehrig became a full-fledged star with 47 home runs, 175 runs batted in, and a .373 batting average; Tony Lazzeri hit .309, Earle Combs .356, and Bob Meusel .337. Led by Waite Hoyt, Herb Pennock, Urban Shocker, and Wilcy Moore, the pitching staff had six men winning in double figures and none losing more than eight games. Overall, the 1927 Yankees won 110 games.

By 1927 Ruth was earning $70,000 a year, a tremendous amount in those preinflation, low-tax days. To give some idea of the heights of that figure, the next highest salary on the club was Earle Combs's $19,500. Lou Gehrig earned $8,000. The average annual salary per man on the greatest team in history was approximately $11,000; take away Ruth's and it was closer to $8,000 per man.

In the National League in 1927 a sharp-hitting Pittsburgh team won the pennant by one and a half games over the de-Hornsbyed Cardinals. The Pirates, hitting as a team at .305, were led by Pie Traynor and the Waner brothers, Paul and Lloyd. Traynor

Four members of the
pitching staff of the 1925
American League pennant-
winning Washington Sena-
tors: **left to right,** Tom
Zachary, Fred Marberry,
Alex Ferguson, and Walter
Johnson.

is generally regarded as the greatest all-around third baseman in
history, with a .320 lifetime batting average and remarkable
defensive skills. (A saying of the time was, "Hornsby doubled twice
down the left field line and each time Traynor threw him out at
first.")

The Waners were a pair of slight, keen-eyed hitters who had
learned how to hit by swinging broom handles at wickedly thrown
corncobs on their father's farm in Harrah, Oklahoma. Paul, the
older, hit .380 in 1927, his second full season in the big leagues,
while rookie Lloyd hit .355. When he retired in 1945, Paul Waner
had a .333 lifetime batting average and was one of only six players
with over 3,000 career hits.

Despite some good hitting by the Waners, the Yankee
steamroller ran over the Pirates in four straight games in the 1927

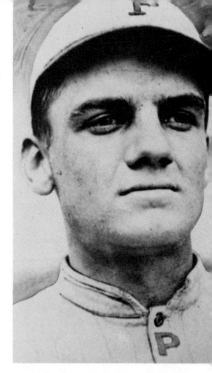

Max Carey of the Pittsburgh Pirates, one of the most prolific base stealers of all time. He led the National League 10 times in stolen bases, with over 700 lifetime.

Roger Peckinpaugh was a fine shortstop for the Yankees and Senators in the twenties. He is, unfortunately, remembered principally for eight errors he made in the 1925 World Series.

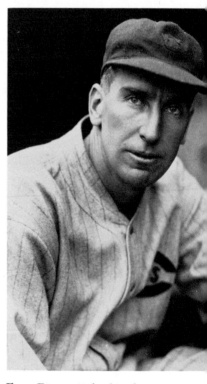

Eppa Rixey pitched in the National League from 1912 through 1933. Four times a 20-game winner, he won 266 games overall.

Dolf Luque was one of the first Latin-American players to make good in a big way in the major leagues. The Cuban-born curve-baller pitched from 1914 through 1935, winning 194 games. In 1923 he won 27 games for Cincinnati.

Outfielder Cy Williams, 19-year National League veteran with the Cubs and Phillies (from 1912 through 1930). He led the league in home runs four times.

Arthur Clarence "Dazzy" Vance, one of the hardest-throwing right-handers of all time. He didn't make it to the major leagues until he was thirty-one years old—but was still there when he was forty-four! Probably the National League's best pitcher in the twenties. In 1924 he won 28 games for the Dodgers.

Wilbert Robinson, Brooklyn's colorful and lovable "Uncle Robbie."

Heinie Manush came to the Detroit Tigers in 1923, listened to batting tips from his manager, Ty Cobb, and went on to play 17 years in the big leagues, finishing with a .330 lifetime batting average.

World Series, with Ruth hitting the only two home runs struck in the Series—which was fitting enough, since the Babe's 60 topped the Pirate's team total of 54. (Ruth, in fact, outhomered 12 of the 16 major league teams in 1927, including every team in the American League.)

In 1928 McGraw's Giants finished two games behind the Cardinals. It was the closest the aging McGraw would come to a pennant again, in spite of a powerful hitting team that included Bill Terry, Travis Jackson, Fred Lindstrom, Lefty O'Doul, Mel Ott, and a solemn young lefty with a deceptive screwball, Carl Hubbell.

The 1928 World Series was a four-game massacre of the Cardinals by the Yankees, headed by a two-man wrecking crew named Ruth and Gehrig; they batted .625 and .545 respectively, with seven home runs between them. It seemed that nothing could stop the Yankees. They had again won three pennants in a row and appeared ready to go on indefinitely.

Rogers Hornsby.

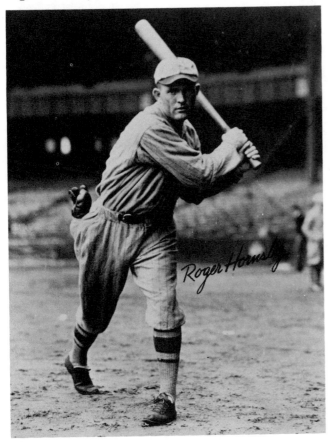

Grover Cleveland Alexander in 1926.

Taylor Douthit, crack center fielder for the pennant-winning Cardinals of 1926 and 1928.

Miller Huggins, when he was playing second base for the St. Louis Cardinals in 1910.

At home plate Chick Hafey hit bullets; in the outfield he threw them. He led the National League with a .349 batting average in 1931. Lifetime, his batting average was .317.

Jimmy Ring, a fireballing right-hander who spent his best years with losing Phillies in the twenties.

Bill Carrigan and Miller Huggins, managers of the Red Sox and Yankees, respectively, in 1927.

Babe Ruth, author and home run hitter, autographing his latest for hospitalized youngsters.

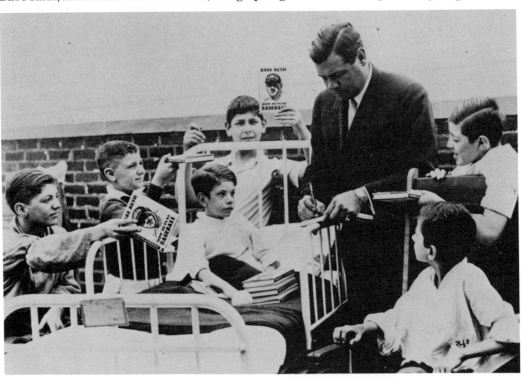

Babe Ruth hitting one against the Pirates in the 1927 World Series.

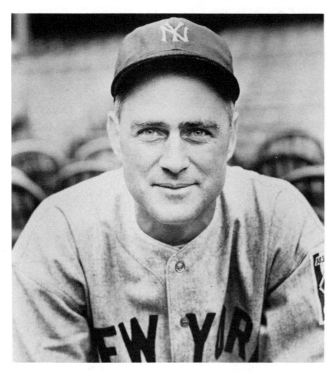

Earle Combs, first of the great Yankee center fielders and one of the standouts of the 1927 Yankees. He batted .356 with 23 triples and 231 hits that year. Spending his entire 12-year career with the Yankees, Combs had a lifetime average of .325.

Herb Pennock, one of the many Red Sox who were sold to the Yankees. Pennock pitched in the American League for 22 years, winning 240 games. He won 5 games and lost none in World Series competition.

Tony Lazzeri, second baseman of the 1927 Yankees. Although he is remembered chiefly today for being struck out by Alexander in the 1926 Series, Lazzeri was a wicked hitter, batting over .300 five times and driving in over 100 runs seven times.

Bob Meusel, rifle-armed left fielder of the 1927 Yankees. The reticent "Silent Bob" hit over .300 seven times, including .337 for the 1927 club. League leader with 33 home runs in 1925. Lifetime batting average: .309.

Fred Lindstrom in the center, flanked by the Waner brothers (Paul, **left**, and Lloyd, **right**).

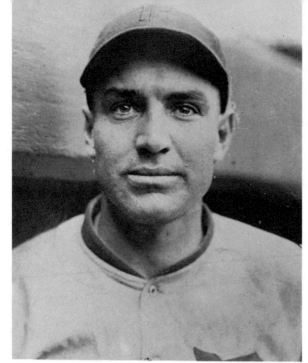

Pittsburgh's Pie Traynor, considered by many the all-time top third baseman. Traynor had 10 years of over-.300 hitting; his peak: .366 in 1930.

Bob "Fats" Fothergill, **left**, and Ted Lyons, **right**. Fothergill was a line-drive hitter for the Tigers in the twenties, hitting over .300 his first eight years in the big leagues. Lyons pitched for the White Sox from 1923 through 1946. Almost always saddled with losing teams, he still won 260 games. Joe McCarthy said that if Ted had pitched for the Yankees he would have won 400.

Glenn Wright, Pittsburgh's stellar shortstop on their pennant winners of 1925 and 1927. A hard hitter who drove in over 100 runs four times, Wright teamed with Traynor to give the Pirates an airtight left side of the infield.

Harry Heilmann.

A familiar ritual: President
Calvin Coolidge about to
throw out the first ball of
the 1928 season. Washing-
ton manager Bucky Harris
is at the right, with
Washington owner Clark
Griffith next to Harris.

Jimmie Foxx. Of one of his drives a bullpen pitcher once said, "We were watching that ball for two innings." He hit them far and he hit them frequently: a lifetime 534 home runs (including 58 in 1932) to go with his lifetime .325 batting average. Thirteen times he drove in over 100 runs, reaching his peak with 175 in 1938.

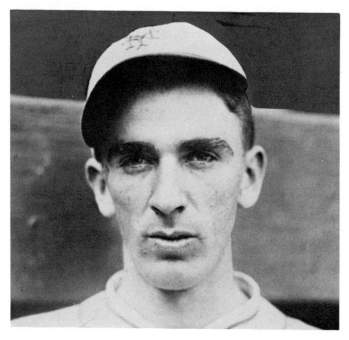

Carl Hubbell in 1928.

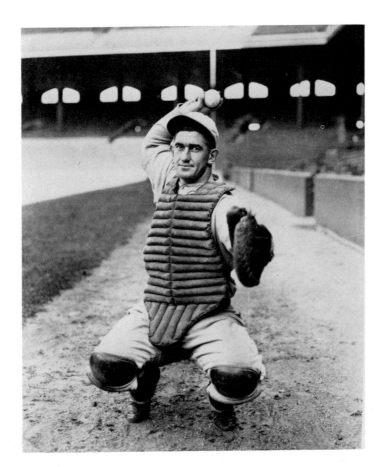

Mickey Cochrane, one of the greatest catchers who ever lived. Cochrane was fiery, aggressive, a natural leader. He batted over .300 eight times. His career came to a premature end when, as player-manager for the Tigers in 1937, he suffered an almost fatal beaning by Yankee pitcher Bump Hadley.

However, the one team considered a rival to the '27 Yankees' accolade of the greatest team ever was ready to emerge and dominate the American League. This was the club that was to become known as the '29-'31 Athletics. Connie Mack's Philadelphia Athletics. The venerable, timeless Connie Mack, winless since dismantling his 1914 team, had patiently put together his greatest team ever. Finishing just two and a half games behind the mighty Yankees in 1928, the Athletics had served notice.

They were headed by some of the finest ballplayers of all time. Their leading hitter was a hot-tempered left-fielder named Al Simmons, who had a peculiar "foot-in-the-bucket" batting stance. Along with Simmons was the man people called the right-handed Babe Ruth—a young, genial powerhouse named Jimmie Foxx. Foxx is the most awesome right-handed power hitter of all time, and his distance hitting is legendary. Behind the plate Mack had

The infield of the 1929-31 Philadelphia Athletics: **left to right**, first baseman Jimmie Foxx, second baseman Max Bishop, shortstop Joe Boley, and third baseman Jimmie Dykes.

Bing Miller.

A pair of rugged .300 hitters who
starred in Connie Mack's outfield in the
last of his glory years.

Mule Haas.

Al Simmons and Babe Ruth at the 1930 World Series. A swaggering man and a savage hitter, Simmons hated all pitchers and his batting averages showed it. He hit over .300 his first 11 years in the big leagues, with peaks of .384 in 1925, .392 in 1927, .381 in 1930, and .390 in 1931—the latter two figures leading the league.

the fiery Mickey Cochrane, a natural leader and one of the best catchers in baseball history. Along with these Titans were infielders Max Bishop, Joe Boley, and Jimmy Dykes, and a pair of .300-hitting outfielders, Mule Haas and Bing Miller.

Mack's pitching was headed by a tempestuous, cantankerous, flamethrowing left-hander, Robert Moses Grove, known as Lefty, whom Mack had purchased from Jack Dunn's Baltimore club for an astonishing $100,600. (The $600 was tacked on to make it the largest minor league purchase ever.) Like Walter Johnson, Grove threw only fastballs, described as "flashing up there like a piece of white thread." Grove's statistics are almost unbelievable. He led the league in strikeouts during his first seven seasons, led in earned run average nine times, won 300 games, and between 1928 and 1931 had a four-year won-lost mark of 103 and 23. Almost as effective as Grove was right-hander George Earnshaw, a steady 20-game winner, and behind Earnshaw was lefty Rube Walberg.

The Athletics won the 1929 American League pennant by 18 games. In the National League a powerful Chicago team, managed by Joe McCarthy, also won easily. McCarthy had a devastating right-handed-hitting lineup, led by Rogers Hornsby batting .380, Riggs Stephenson .362, Kiki Cuyler .360, and home run slugger Hack Wilson who hit only .345. Pat Malone, Charlie Root, and Guy Bush led McCarthy's fine pitching staff. The 1929 World Series promised to be a thriller.

It was the preponderance of the Cubs' right-handed lineup that

Robert Moses Grove.

Lefty Grove receiving a silver cup for having been voted the American League's Most Valuable Player in 1931, the year he won 31 games and lost only 4.

George Earnshaw ranked right behind Grove on Connie Mack's pitching staff. The big right-hander won 24, 22, and 21 games in the pennant years 1929-31.

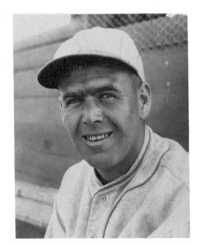

Howard Ehmke.

George Earnshaw (left) and Jimmie Dykes helping Mr. Mack celebrate his sixty-ninth birthday in 1931.

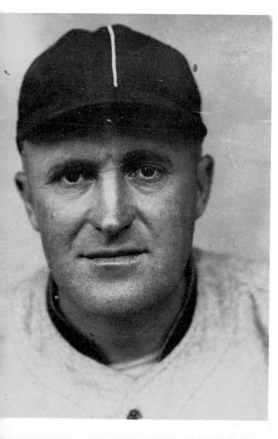

Joe McCarthy, manager of the Chicago Cubs, in 1929. Through the years he managed such greats as Rogers Hornsby, Babe Ruth, Lou Gehrig, Joe DiMaggio, and Ted Williams, among many, many others. McCarthy himself played 15 years in the minors but never a day in the big leagues.

Guy Bush, for many years one of the Cubs' pitching aces.

One of the most talented outfielders in the twenties and thirties, Hazen Shirley "Kiki" Cuyler hit over .350 four times and four times led the National League in stolen bases.

Charlie Grimm. Remembered primarily as a manager (he won three pennants with the Cubs) and as a raconteur, Charlie was also for many years one of the best first basemen in the National League.

It was the preponderance of the Cubs' right-handed lineup that led Mack into a daring opening-game move in the 1929 Series. He started veteran right-hander Howard Ehmke, winner of only seven games all year, bypassing both Grove and Earnshaw. Not only did Ehmke's slow-breaking balls baffle the Chicago sluggers, but the veteran also established a World Series record for the time with 13 strikeouts. "Connie taught me a lesson that time," an admiring McCarthy said years later.

Mack never did start the great Lefty Grove in the Series, holding him back as a relief pitcher. Connie, in fact, started George Earnshaw in two consecutive games, with only a day's rest. The

Athletics won two of the first three games. Then came number four and the most memorable rally in World Series history. Going into the bottom of the seventh inning, the Cubs were leading 8-0 and seemed about to tie the Series at two games apiece. Parlaying some misplayed fly balls in the outfield with a barrage of base hits, however, the A's scored 10 runs in the seventh inning. Lefty Grove walked out of the bullpen to pitch the eighth and ninth. Grove faced six men, fanned four of them, and the Athletics had a 3-1 edge in the Series.

When Philadelphia came to bat in the bottom of the ninth inning of the fifth game they were losing, 2-0. With one out, Max Bishop singled, Mule Haas homered to tie the score, Mickey Cochrane grounded out, Al Simmons doubled, Jimmie Foxx was walked intentionally, and then Bing Miller doubled home the winning run. The 1929 World Series was over in a flash of lightning and a roll of thunder.

"Boy," Lefty Grove said later, "some ball club, huh?"

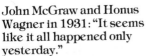

John McGraw and Honus Wagner in 1931: "It seems like it all happened only yesterday."

Hack Wilson.

Bill Terry, New York Giants' first baseman and McGraw's successor as Giant manager. He batted .401 in 1930.

Lefty O'Doul's big league career was short but sweet. Playing only six full seasons, he hit .349 lifetime (fourth highest in history). In 1929 he led the National League with a .398 batting average.

Depression and Innovation

1930-1939

IN 1930 the gloom of an economic depression was beginning to cast a pall over the land. Everything, it seemed, was sinking and deflating—except the batting averages in the National League. Playing with a hyped-up ball, the league went on a batting rampage that tore whole pages from the record books.

Giants' first baseman Bill Terry led the league in 1930 with a .401 batting average, followed by Brooklyn's Babe Herman at .393 and a pair of Philly outfielders, Chuck Klein and Lefty O'Doul, at .386 and .383 respectively. Overall, the National League batted .303, headed by the Giants' remarkable team average of .319. Amazingly, the Philadelphia Phillies had a team batting average of .315 and finished dead last!

Chicago Cubs' outfielder Hack Wilson set a league record with 56 home runs and an all-time runs-batted-in record of 190. For the second year in a row the Chicago outfield of Hack Wilson, Kiki Cuyler, and Riggs Stephenson averaged over .350. Hack Wilson was a stocky little muscleman who possessed great capacities for hitting, friendship, and beer. A promising player with McGraw's Giants some years earlier, Wilson had been farmed out for more experience. Through a clerical error in the Giants' front office, he was left exposed to the baseball draft and quickly grabbed by the Cubs for a few thousand dollars. When McGraw heard what had happened, his rage was monumental; but there was nothing he could do about it. Wilson was gone.

Chuck Klein, a powerhouse for the Philadelphia Phillies, had 200 or more hits his first five full seasons in the major leagues. In 1933 he led the league with a .368 batting average.

Hack was 5 feet 6 inches tall, weighed 195 pounds, and could hit a baseball prodigious distances. He played with verve and enthusiasm and was a tremendous favorite with the fans. However, he was not always in the best of condition. The story is told that one day he was patrolling right field when his team's pitcher was getting hit unmercifully by the opposition. Line drives were caroming off the outfield fence above Hack's head one after the other, and he was getting exhausted running them down, especially since he hadn't slept too much the night before. A welcome pause came in the action as the manager came to the mound to change pitchers, and Hack took advantage of the breather out in right field. He rested as best he could, his hands on his knees, staring down at the grass, trying to catch his wind. But the unhappy pitcher, instead of handing the ball to his successor, angrily threw it against the right field fence with all his might. Hearing the ball hit the fence Hack thought the game had resumed: as the crowd watched in surprise he raced after the ball as fast as he could, retrieved it, and fired it back into second base—a perfect peg to get the runner, if only there had been one!

The manager of the Chicago Cubs, the notoriously strict Joe McCarthy, handled the fun-loving Hack with great skill. "You can do what you want off the field," McCarthy told his slugger, "as long as you keep hitting. If you stop hitting, you're in trouble." Wilson stopped hitting the next year, but by that time McCarthy was managing the Yankees—much to the displeasure of Babe Ruth, who had been casting his eye on the job. Ruth became openly hostile to McCarthy, who "handled" the aging slugger by ignoring him.

McCarthy's favorite player throughout his long career as Yankee manager was the remarkably durable Lou Gehrig, whose frightening power and 2,130 consecutive-game playing streak are of mythic proportions. The New York-born Gehrig was a modest man whose joys in life were fishing, smoking his pipe, and hitting blistering line drives to all fields. Once, when one of his managers, Bob Shawkey, chewed him out for some inept footwork around first base that cost the Yankees a game, the sensitive Gehrig turned to his locker and wept.

When he first joined the Yankees, Gehrig idolized Ruth. Lou, who had attended Columbia University for a time, was called by the rough-humored Ruth a "kink-headed college kid" among other things. The quiet, smiling Gehrig tolerated Ruth's jibes without retort. They remained friends for years, teammates and bridge partners. Stardom, however, gradually turned the basically conservative Gehrig into a more and more serious man, even a stuffy one, a stern upholder of the Yankee image (he would frown at those teammates who did not meet his standard of Yankee dignity).

Eventually, one might say inevitably, a rift developed between Gehrig and Ruth, and the two did not speak for years. There was, however, an emotional reunion between the two all-time Yankee greats on Lou Gehrig Appreciation Day at Yankee Stadium on July 4, 1939, when tribute was paid to the fatally ill Gehrig, who then had less than two years to live.

It seemed to be Gehrig's fate to live in the shadow of others. The first half of his career was played in Ruth's shadow, the final years in DiMaggio's. Even on his greatest day, June 3, 1932, when he hit four home runs in a game against the Athletics, the headlines went to John McGraw—who chose that day to announce his retirement as manager of the Giants.

In 1932 Gehrig had a sensational four-game World Series against the Chicago Cubs, batting .529 and hitting three home runs. But again Ruth stole the show. For it was what the Babe did—or didn't do—in the third game in Wrigley Field that will always dominate the 1932 World Series.

There was bad blood between the Yankees and the Chicago Cubs even before the 1932 Series started. Late in the season Chicago shortstop Billy Jurges had suffered an injury, and the Cubs dug into the minor leagues and came up with ex-Yankee Mark Koenig to replace him. Playing superbly, Koenig helped the Cubs to a pennant. When it came to dividing the World Series money, however, Koenig was voted just a half share by his teammates. This rankled many of his old friends on the Yankees, particularly Ruth, to whom parsimony was unforgivable.

The exchange of insults between the Yankees and Cubs grew increasingly more heated and rancorous. By the middle of the third game there was considerable bitterness between Ruth and the Cubs. In the top of the fifth inning Ruth walked to the plate with one out, the bases empty, and the score tied, 4-4. The invective coming from the Cubs' bench was savage and obscene. Charlie Root, the Chicago pitcher, got two quick strikes across. What happened then has been, and will forever be, a matter of controversy.

Ruth made some sort of gesture: the Cubs said he was holding up one finger and pointing out at Root to indicate he still had one strike left; some of Babe's teammates insisted he was pointing out to the center field bleachers, showing where he was going to hit Root's next pitch. Whatever he was doing then, there was no doubt about what he did a moment later—he hit a tremendous home run over the bleacher screen in center field.

Did he call his shot or didn't he? Ruth claimed—after the fact—that he had. The Cubs scoffed at the idea. But it really does not matter. Like so many other things involving George Herman Ruth, the truth has been covered by the gentle mists of legend. There are certain things that seem to please history, and the chances are that history will have it that Babe Ruth indeed "called" the home run that proved to be his last in World Series competition.

The 1932 Cubs had put a stop to a two-year surge by the St. Louis Cardinals, National League pennant winners in 1930 and 1931. St. Louis was led by Jim Bottomley, the rifle-armed Chick Hafey, and the man described by Joe McCarthy in 1932 as the game's best all-around player—Frankie Frisch. The '31 Cardinals in turn had beaten the Athletics in the World Series and thus derailed Connie Mack in his quest for a third consecutive World Championship. The prime factor in the the 1931 World Series was a Cardinal rookie outfielder named Pepper Martin.

Dazzy Vance pitching to Kiki Cuyler at Ebbets Field in the summer of 1930. Note that the famous right field scoreboard had not yet been built, nor the double-deck stands in center field.

Lou Gehrig.

Lou Gehrig after hitting his last World
Series home run (against the Giants in
1937). The Giants' catcher is Harry
Danning.

Babe Herman and son Billy at the 1933 All-Star game in Chicago. In 1929 and 1930 Herman's batting averages were .381 and .393.

Seldom in history has a single player so thoroughly dominated a World Series. Pepper Martin, an Oklahoma greyhound of engaging simplicity, had 12 hits in 24 times at bat, including four doubles and a home run. He also stole five bases, running primarily on Grove and Earnshaw. Midway through the Series, when he had already become a national hero, an admiring Judge Landis said, with normal fan-envy, "How I'd love to change places with you, Martin." To this the blithe Pepper answered, "Fine with me, Judge, if you're willing to swap your fifty thousand a year for my forty-five hundred."

Gabby Hartnett, the Chicago Cubs' great catcher, and Charlie Root, the man who did or did not throw that famous pitch to Babe Ruth in the 1932 Series.

One of the pitchers Martin tattooed in that Series was the mighty Lefty Grove, who reached his peak that year with 31 wins and 4 losses. It was around this time that a plate-glass manufacturer produced what they proudly claimed was a shatter-proof product. Deciding to put the glass to the supreme test, they carried several sheets of it to Philadelphia's Shibe Park and asked the fastest pitcher in baseball to throw at it. Grove's first pitch went right through it, like a bullet, leaving a baseball-sized hole. Chagrined, the manufacturer asked Lefty to ease up a little. They trundled out another sheet, stood it up, and told Grove to throw again. The second pitch hit the glass like a bomb, shattering it into a thousand pieces. The choleric Grove walked away muttering, while the glass people returned to the drawing board.

Connie Mack's last dynasty ended in 1932, when the Athletics finished 13 games behind the Yankees, despite Jimmie Foxx's 58 home runs and Lefty Grove's 25 wins. Under increasing financial pressure, caused by dwindling attendance and stock market losses, Mack again dismantled a great ball club. Grove and Foxx were sold to the Red Sox; Simmons, Dykes, Haas, and Earnshaw to the White Sox; Cochrane to Detroit. Although he would later bring up some fine hitters in Doc Cramer, Pinky Higgins, and Bob Johnson, Mack would win no more pennants.

Manager Joe McCarthy's bid to get another Yankee dynasty in high gear was derailed for several years, first by the Washington Senators in 1933 and then by a powerful Detroit team in 1934 and 1935. Under player-manager Mickey Cochrane, the Detroit Tigers fielded a strong, well-balanced club. Along with the fiery Cochrane, Detroit had a slugging young first baseman named Hank Greenberg, the superlative Charlie Gehringer at second, and heavy-hitting outfielders Goose Goslin, Pete Fox, and Gerald Walker. On

Billy Herman, the Cubs' second baseman in the thirties. A lifetime .304 hitter, Herman led the league with 227 hits in 1935. In the forties he starred with the Dodgers.

Judge Landis and pitcher Burleigh Grimes exchanging pleasantries during the 1930 World Series.

Sunny Jim Bottomley, first baseman on the St. Louis Cardinals' all-.300-hitting lineup in 1930. Bottomley holds the major league record with 12 runs batted in in a single game, on September 16, 1924.

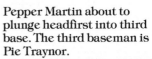

Pepper Martin.

Pepper Martin about to plunge headfirst into third base. The third baseman is Pie Traynor.

Lou Gehrig, Jimmie Foxx, and Babe Ruth in the early thirties.

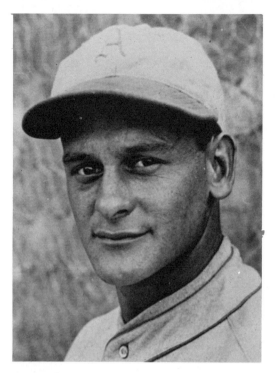

"Indian Bob" Johnson. Part Cherokee and all hitter, Johnson drove in over 100 runs seven straight seasons for Connie Mack, from 1935 through 1941.

Pinky Higgins, Mack's sharp-hitting third baseman in the early thirties. Higgins is coholder, with Walt Dropo, of the major league record for hitting safely in consecutive times at bat: in 1938, he got 12 consecutive base hits.

Doc Cramer took over center field for Mack after Connie broke up the great '29-'31 team. A model of consistency, Cramer played for 20 years, finishing with a .296 lifetime batting average.

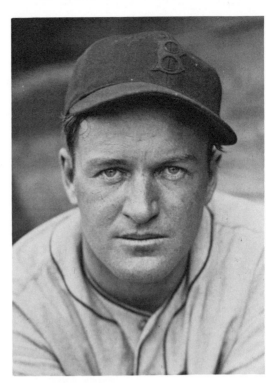

Joe Cronin, one of the hardest-hitting shortstops of all time. Cronin was also player-manager for Washington and the Boston Red Sox. Eight times he drove in over 100 runs.

It is August 26, 1934, and pitcher Schoolboy Rowe (sitting) has just won his sixteenth straight game with the help of a ninth-inning home run by Hank Greenberg (shaking hands). Rowe was defeated the next time out and remains coholder of the American League record for consecutive wins with Walter Johnson, Smoky Joe Wood, and Lefty Grove.

Detroit's Hank Greenberg, one of the mightiest of power hitters. Four times the American League's home run leader, he hit his peak with 58 in 1938. In 1937 he drove in 183 runs.

Tommy Bridges, possessor of one of the finest curve balls of his era, and a 20-game winner for Detroit in 1934, '35, and '36.

Detroit's "Mechanical Man," the quiet, deadly efficient Charlie Gehringer, one of the greatest second basemen of all time. He led the league with a .371 batting average in 1937. During 16 full seasons, he batted over .300 thirteen times.

Alvin Crowder, one of the aces of Detroit's 1935 pennant winners. Previously, he had won 26 games for Washington in 1932, and 24 in 1933.

Goose Goslin.

Some heavy lumber in Detroit's 1934 outfield. **Left to right:** Gee Walker, Jo-Jo White, Goose Goslin, and Pete Fox.

the mound the Tigers had 20-game winners Schoolboy Rowe (who won 16 straight games in 1934) and curve-baller Tommy Bridges..

Detroit's opponents in the 1934 World Series were the rambunctious St. Louis Cardinals, led by a laughing, mischievous, fireballing twenty-three-year-old right-hander named Dizzy Dean, who was about to replace the fading Babe Ruth as the game's premier gate attraction. A practical joker of note, Dean and a teammate once entertained themselves on a rainy day in their Philadelphia hotel by donning overalls and, carrying paint buckets and ladders, invaded the ballroom where a convention was being held. They solemnly announced that the place was to be painted. When the upset conventioneers realized who their tormentor was, a great cheer went up and Dean was invited to make a speech.

A pair of 30-game winners shake hands before the 1936 All-Star game. Lefty Grove, **left**, and Dizzy Dean.

Dizzy Dean signing autographs for some of his fans.

——▶ Action in the first game of the 1934 World Series: Detroit's Goose Goslin is tagged out at second by the Cardinals' Frankie Frisch. Shortstop Leo Durocher is in the background. The umpire is Harry Geisel.

Paul Dean. Two 19-game seasons and then, at the age of twenty-two, a sore arm.

——▶ The 1934 World Series, two days later. This time it is Frisch who is out at second as Charlie Gehringer fires the ball to first to complete a double play. The umpire is Brick Owens.

The 1934 World Series, game four, fourth inning. Dizzy Dean went in as a pinch runner. The next batter, Pepper Martin, hit a double-play ball to Gehringer, **right**, who threw to shortstop Billy Rogell, who fired on to first. Dean came in to second base standing up. He did not stand up long; Rogell's throw hit him in the head and he is about to go down. Dizzy was carried off the field on a stretcher, but he showed up at the hotel that night brimming with the deathless line: "They X-rayed my head and didn't find anything."

Joe Medwick.

A trio of heavy-hitting Chicago Cubs' outfielders in 1933. **Left to right:** Riggs Stephenson, Kiki Cuyler, Babe Herman. Lifetime batting averages: Stephenson .336, Cuyler .321, Herman .324.

One of the finest batteries in Chicago Cubs' history: catcher Gabby Hartnett, **left,** and pitcher Lon Warneke.

Outfielder Earl Averill of the
Cleveland Indians: lifetime batting
average, .318. Averill was one of the
most popular players ever to wear a
Cleveland uniform; his best year was
1936 when he hit .378.

Wes Ferrell: handsome, hot-
tempered, and a winner. Six
times Ferrell won 20 games
or more, including his first
four years in the big leagues
(still a record). Ferrell was
also a heavy hitter—his 38
home runs are still the
record for a pitcher.

Cleveland's Mel Harder and the Cardinals' Bill
Walker at the 1935 All-Star game in Cleveland.
Harder won 223 games for the Indians over a 20-
year career. Walker twice led National League
pitchers in earned run average.

Luke Appling, a 20-year man at shortstop for the Chicago White Sox and a perennial .300 hitter. In 1936 he hit his peak with a .388 batting average, leading the American League. He won a second batting crown in 1943 with a mark of .328.

In 1934, Dean, earning a depression-era salary of $6,500, won 30 games and lost 7 for a rough-and-tumble St. Louis club that was to become known as the Gas House Gang. Featured members were Dean, player-manager Frankie Frisch, first baseman Rip Collins, shortstop Leo Durocher, Pepper Martin, and a sullen mass of muscles who hit smoking line drives in all directions, Joe Medwick. Medwick was to become the National League's top hitter in the late thirties, winning the Triple Crown in 1937 with 31 home runs, 154 runs batted in, and a .374 batting average.

Before the 1934 World Series, Dean announced that he and his brother Paul (who was known as Daffy) would beat the Tigers all by themselves. Paul Dean had won 19 games for the Cardinals and was considered by some a harder thrower than his older brother. Dizzy's prediction stood up. Dizzy and Daffy handcuffed Detroit's powerhouse lineup and won two games apiece in the seven-game Series.

Dizzy Dean's career has been likened to the dramatic suddenness, glow, and abrupt disappearance of a comet. He

Arky Vaughan, next to Honus Wagner probably the greatest all-around shortstop in National League history. Vaughan hit over .300 his first 10 years in the big leagues, leading the league with a .385 batting average in 1935. His .318 lifetime batting average is higher than any shortstop in the Hall of Fame, with the exception of Wagner.

Carl Hubbell in the thirties.

Gus Mancuso caught for 17 years in the National League, mostly with the Giants.

followed his 30-game season in 1934 with winning totals of 28 and 24, and was rolling along in high gear when he suffered an injury in the 1937 All-Star game that was to lead to his premature fall from stardom. Pitching to Cleveland's Earl Averill, Dean was struck on the foot by a line drive and suffered a broken toe. He resumed pitching before the toe was fully healed and, favoring the injury, deviated from his natural style of delivery and hurt his arm. Almost overnight the smoke left his fastball.

In 1938 canny Branch Rickey, the Cardinals' general manager, sold the dead-armed Dean to the Chicago Cubs for $185,000 plus several players. Dizzy won a handful of games for the Cubs over the next three years, then faded from the diamond—only to reappear years later as a popular announcer who mangled the King's English on television's "Game of the Week." "The runner slud into third base," Diz would say, or "It's a foul ball and the base runners have to return to their respectable bases." He meant "to their respective bases" and the fans across America loved it.

Freddie Fitzsimmons, fine knuckleball pitcher for the Giants and Dodgers from 1925 through 1943.

Mel Ott. Joining the Giants as a seventeen-year-old in 1926, Ott remained for 23 years as player and manager. Despite his high kick at the plate, Ott could not be pitched to. A sharp pull hitter, the short right field wall at the Polo Grounds was made to order for him. He had a lifetime total of 511 home runs, leading the league six times.

Mel Ott and Lou Gehrig.

Terry Moore, one of the greatest defensive center fielders of all time.

Van Lingle Mungo, one of the hardest throwers in National League history. Mungo was Brooklyn's ace through most of the thirties.

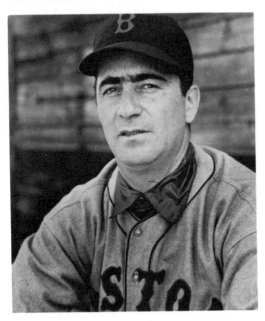

Moe Berg, probably the most erudite man ever to play in the big leagues. A fine catcher with a weak bat, it was said of Berg that "he could speak eleven languages but couldn't hit in any of them."

Charlie Dressen. After a nondescript career as a third baseman with Cincinnati, Chuck Dressen turned to managing. Considered a highly perceptive baseball man, he won pennants with the Brooklyn Dodgers in 1952 and 1953, but was released when he demanded a contract for more than one year. Walter Alston thereupon took over and remained the Dodgers' manager for 23 years—always with one-year contracts.

Three members of the Gas House Gang in repose. Left to right: outfielder-third baseman Pepper Martin, catcher Mickey Owen, and pitcher Lon Warneke.

Dean's only rival for supremacy of the National League mounds in the 1930s was a pitcher who was his opposite in every conceivable way. Carl Hubbell was left-handed, poker-faced, modest, and instead of speed he threw a sharp-breaking screwball that baffled opposing batters. Hubbell pitched Bill Terry's New York Giants into the World Series in 1933, 1936, and 1937.

From 1933 through 1937, Hubbell won 115 games and lost 50. Over the 1936-37 seasons he won 24 consecutive games. In 1933 King Carl went 46 consecutive innings without yielding a run. On July 2, 1933, he pitched 18 innings in beating the Cardinals, 1-0, surrendering six hits and no bases on balls!

George Case, base stealer extraordinaire. One of the fastest men of his era, he led the league in stolen bases six times.

Buddy Myer was another consistent .300 hitter for Washington in the 1930s. A rough and tough second baseman, he led the American League with a .349 batting average in 1935.

Cecil Travis. Year after year a .300 hitter for the Washington Senators. His best: .359 in 1941.

Outfielder-third baseman Buddy Lewis of the Washington Senators, another fine hitter.

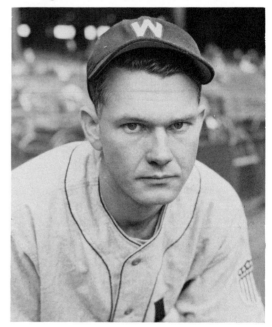

Stanley "Frenchy" Bordagaray caused a scandal when he came to spring training in 1936 wearing this modest mustache. A man ahead of his time, he was forced to shave it off. A colorful and likable man, Frenchy once lost his head and spit at an umpire. When he saw the size of his fine, he said, "It was more than I expectorated."

Rudy York, power-hitting first baseman for the Detroit Tigers. Checking his glove in the background is Charlie Gehringer.

Mickey Cochrane being
carried off the field at Yankee
Stadium after his near-fatal
beaning by Bump Hadley on
May 25, 1937.

John Henry "Zeke" Bonura,
heavy-hitting White Sox first
baseman. Lifetime batting
average: .307.

But Carl Hubbell's most memorable moment came in the 1934 All-Star game, which he started for the National League. Hubbell opened the game inauspiciously, yielding a single to Charlie Gehringer and walking Heinie Manush. The next three hitters were Babe Ruth, Lou Gehrig, and Jimmie Foxx—the greatest three-man concentration of power ever to appear in one lineup. The Giants' master craftsman calmly fanned each with his screwball. Then he began the second inning by striking out Al Simmons and Joe Cronin, before Bill Dickey broke the spell with a single. Hubbell's performance in the '34 All-Star game remains one of the pitching highlights in baseball history.

Baseball struggled on through the depression, a source of diversion for a troubled people. Cleveland ace Wes Ferrell, after setting a record by winning 20 or more games his first four years, was forced to take a $7,000 salary cut. "Even then," Ferrell recalled, "I was still driving a better car than the club owner."

In an effort to stimulate attendance, an unpredictable visionary named Leland Stanford "Larry" MacPhail brought baseball its most telling innovation: on May 24, 1935, MacPhail, general manager of the Cincinnati Reds, introduced night baseball to the major leagues. The idea had been resisted by the game's conservative owners, who did not feel the fans would accept it. In the beginning, they limited MacPhail to just seven games per season under his newly installed lights, one with each team in the league. Fan response to night ball, however, proved immediate and enthusiastic. MacPhail later moved on to head the Brooklyn Dodgers and, after the war, bought an interest in the Yankees, bringing night ball with him. By 1948 every park in the major leagues, with the exception of Chicago's Wrigley Field, had installed lights.

Al Lopez caught in the big leagues for 19 years and then went on to manage for another 16.

Gabby Hartnett after his famous home run in the gloaming against the Pirates on September 28, 1938.

Baseball's other front-office genius in the 1930s was the erudite, cigar-smoking, Bible-quoting general manager of the Cardinals, Branch Rickey. Rickey has been given credit for originating baseball's "farm system," which he began for the Cardinals after the First World War. Rickey's method was to sign any youth who showed the merest flash of talent and send him out somewhere to the Cardinals' vast network of minor league clubs, which at one time numbered over 50 teams and some 800 ballplayers. Signing the eager youngsters for as little as $60 a month, Rickey's system was to find quality in quantity. Over the years the Cardinal "chain gang" produced a seemingly endless flow of talent, including players like Chick Hafey, Dizzy Dean, Joe Medwick, Johnny Mize, Pete Reiser, Enos Slaughter, Terry Moore, Marty Marion, Mort and Walker Cooper, Stan Musial, and literally hundreds of others, many of whom the shrewd Rickey developed at a pittance and later sold for substantial sums to other clubs.

Bill Lee. Lee won 20 games or more in each of the Cubs' pennant years of 1935 and 1938.

Hand third base to a man like Stan Hack and you won't have to worry about that position for 15 years. Between 1934 and 1946 Hack never hit below .282 nor above .323.

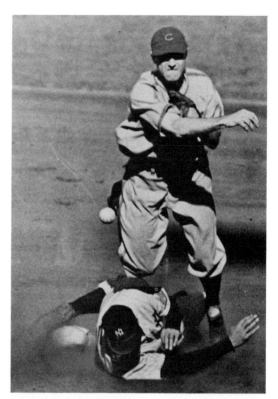

Action in the 1938 World Series. Cubs' shortstop Billy Jurges is firing to first base to complete a double play. The sliding runner is Joe DiMaggio.

Rip Radcliff, outfielder and hitter. Lifetime batting average: .311.

Hal Trosky, one of the great power hitters in Cleveland history. His best year was 1936, when he hit 42 home runs, batted .343, and led the league with 162 runs batted in.

Joe Vosmik, one of the heavy guns in Cleveland's attack in the thirties. In 1935 he hit .348 and led the league in hits, doubles, and triples.

Harlond Clift, third baseman for the St. Louis
Browns. He drove in 118
runs in 1937 and again in
1938.

Claude Passeau led the
National League in strikeouts in 1939. He pitched a
one-hitter against Detroit
in the 1945 World Series.

Double-No-Hit Johnny Vander Meer, shown here with his manager,
Bill McKechnie, left, and his catcher, Ernie Lombardi.

Ironically, the day after the introduction of night ball saw the
last great day of Babe Ruth. The now forty-year-old slugger had
been released by the Yankees after the 1934 season and signed by
the Boston Braves. Babe Ruth had at last proved to be mortal. At
forty he was fat, slow, and could no longer run, field, or swing the
bat with his old authority. On May 25, 1935, however, the legend
rose from its own ruins with one final surge. On that day the Babe
momentarily recaptured his glory days at Forbes Field in
Pittsburgh with three mighty home runs—the last one clearing the
right-field roof and declared the longest drive ever hit in that park.
Shortly after, Babe Ruth, batting .181, retired.

Bucky Walters.

Paul Derringer.

Cincinnati's pitching wizards on their 1939 and 1940 pennant winners. Walters, a converted infielder, won 27 and 22 games during those years, leading the league in earned run average each time. Derringer won 25 and 20 in the pennant years. They each won two games against Detroit in the 1940 World Series.

Ernie Lombardi's famous "snooze" at home plate in the fourth and final game of the 1939 World Series against the Yankees. What actually happened was that Yankee runner Charlie Keller accidentally hit Cincinnati catcher Lombardi in the head with his knee as he scored, stunning the big catcher. Seeing Lombardi lying there dazed, an alert Joe DiMaggio raced home from third. Pitcher Bucky Walters is on the right. The umpire is Babe Pinelli.

With an efficiency that was to prove typical of them, the Yankees were able to replace the irreplaceable. Less than a year after the departure of Ruth, they purchased from San Francisco of the Pacific Coast League—for $25,000 and several minor league players—a twenty-year-old outfielder who was to become the finest all-around baseball-playing machine of the age: Joe DiMaggio.

Born to play center field, the shy, inscrutable DiMaggio was the flawless ballplayer. (One purist once asked Joe McCarthy whether or not DiMaggio could bunt. "I don't know," the Yankee manager responded, "nor have I any intention of ever finding out.") He ranged in center field with unerring judgment and poetic grace. His arm was powerful and accurate. At the plate he had no weakness, and not even the vast reaches of Yankee Stadium's left and center fields could neutralize his tremendous right-handed power.

Quiet, aloof, undemonstrative, DiMaggio became the very embodiment of Yankee pride. Playing without complaint through frequent pain and injury, he was idolized by his teammates and respected by his opponents. With DiMaggio as its centerpiece, the New York Yankee dynasty began a resurgence that would bring 22 pennants in 29 years. Benefiting from a farm system overseen by the shrewd George Weiss, the Yankees soon had a roster stocked with home-grown ballplayers such as Charlie Keller, Joe Gordon, Phil Rizzuto, Spud Chandler, and others.

From 1936 through 1939 the Yankees averaged over 100 wins a season, won four American League pennants, and an unprecedented four straight World Championships. Along with their powerful hitting, the Yankees also boasted fine pitching, headed by two veterans, Red Ruffing and Lefty Gomez. Gomez was a fastballing left-hander and one of the game's fine wits. One day he was the victim of a mammoth Jimmie Foxx home run into the upper reaches of Yankee Stadium's left-field stands. When asked how far the ball had gone, Gomez replied, "I don't know how far it went, but it takes forty-five minutes to walk up there." Upon another occasion, when asked to what he attributed his success, Gomez responded with a classic line: "Clean living and a fast outfield."

DiMaggio was one of a triumvirate of exceptionally gifted youngsters who were to enter baseball in the latter part of the decade. The same year that he joined the Yankees saw the entrance into the American League of baseball's first and thus far only prodigy, a seventeen-year-old Iowa farmboy who fired the most lethal fastball since Walter Johnson.

Detroit's Rudy York and the
Yankees' Charlie Keller.

Robert William Andrew Feller was discovered by Cleveland
scout Cy Slapnicka. Slapnicka was heading west to scout pitcher
Claude Passeau in the minor leagues and stopped off in Iowa to
look at Feller as a favor to some local people who had been writing
him letters about the youngster. Slapnicka took one look and
immediately signed the boy for a grand bonus of an autographed
ball and one dollar. This was in June 1935. A little over a year later
Feller was America's most famous teen-ager. (The overwhelmed
Slapnicka never did get out to see Passeau.)

Bob Feller stayed with the Indians as a nonroster player
through the first half of 1936. In midseason, Cleveland had an
exhibition game booked with the St. Louis Cardinals, the mighty
Gas House Gang. The Indians scheduled Feller to pitch the first
three innings. When St. Louis player-manager Frank Frisch saw
the high-kicking youngster firing his warmups, he promptly
reached for the lineup card, erased his own name, and penciled in
that of a utility infielder. Frisch would have none of it. The

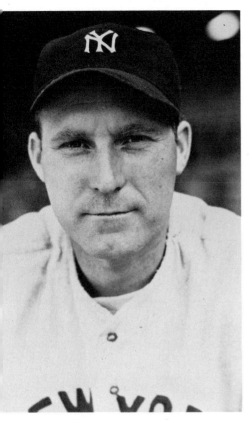

Red Ruffing, who won 20 or more games during each of the Yankees' four championship years, 1936 through 1939.

Bill Dickey, the Yankees' incomparable catcher. Lifetime batting average: .313. His peak year was 1936, when he hit .362.

Red Rolfe, third baseman for the Yankees in the thirties. In 1939 he hit .329 and led the league with 213 hits and 46 doubles.

Cardinals' manager then sat back and with a mixture of chagrin and admiration watched the unknown farmboy speed his fastball and break his lethal curve for three innings, striking out eight of the astonished Cardinals.

Cleveland then put Feller on the roster, breaking the youngster in gradually. Finally, on August 23, 1936, Feller was given his first starting assignment, against the St. Louis Browns. His performance was electrifying. Feller struck out 15, one short of Rube Waddell's American League record and two short of Dizzy Dean's major league record, set in 1933. Three weeks later he tied Dean when he fanned 17 Philadelphia Athletics. "That hit the newspapers like thunder and lightning," Feller said later, "and I guess that's when people began to realize I was for real."

On October 3, 1938, the last day of the season, Detroit's Hank Greenberg had 58 home runs and a clear shot at Ruth's record of 60. In anticipation of baseball history being made, newsreel cameras were on the scene. Baseball history was indeed made that afternoon but not by Greenberg. On that October afternoon a blazing Bob Feller struck out 18 Tigers and set a new stikeout record. The best that Greenberg could manage against the nineteen-year-old Feller was a double in four times at bat, striking out twice. Ironically, Feller lost his great game, 4-1, giving up seven hits and seven walks between his strikeouts.

However, the tail end of the 1938 season did see one of the game's most dramatic home runs, even though it wasn't hit by Hank Greenberg. The Chicago Cubs and Pittsburgh Pirates were battling for the National League pennant when Pittsburgh came to Wrigley Field for a decisive series, one and a half games ahead. The Cubs won the first game to move within one-half game of the top.

The next day the two teams went into the bottom of the ninth tied, 5-5. With darkness falling, a tie seemed fated, necessitating a doubleheader the next day, a disadvantage for a worn-out Chicago pitching staff. With two out and the bases empty in the bottom of the ninth, and little daylight left, Chicago player-manager Gabby Hartnett stepped to the plate. Pirate reliever Mace Brown whipped across two strikes. Brown's next pitch was a fastball that Hartnett drove into the left-field bleachers—the famous "home run in the gloaming." The blow gave the Cubs the game and first place. They beat the demoralized Pirates again the next day and went on to win the pennant.

On June 15, 1938, Larry MacPhail brought night ball to Ebbets Field in Brooklyn. The debut proved spectacular. Four days before, on June 11, Cincinnati's wild, hard-throwing left-hander, Johnny Vander Meer, had hurled a no-hitter against the Boston

Lefty Gomez, the Yankees' ace left-hander and reigning wit. Four times a 20-game winner, Gomez's best year was 1934 when he won 26 games, leading the league in earned run average, strikeouts, shutouts, complete games, and winning percentage. In World Series competition he was perfect, winning six and losing none.

The day it ended for Lou
Gehrig: Detroit, May 2,
1939. Sitting next to Lou on
the dugout steps is Lefty
Gomez.

Braves. His next start was under Brooklyn's brand-new lighting
system. Vander Meer inaugurated night ball in Brooklyn with what
remains an unparalleled performance—a second consecutive no-
hitter. Pitching under incredible pressure, Vander Meer walked the
bases loaded in the ninth inning. Reaching back and firing with
everything he had, he achieved the game's final out when Dodger
shortstop Leo Durocher lifted an easy fly to center field.

Baseball's most remarkable endurance streak came to an end
on May 2, 1939, when Yankee first baseman Lou Gehrig took

Manager Joe McCarthy.

Bob Feller. His statistics are astonishing: six times a 20-game winner, seven times leading the league in strikeouts, five times in shutouts, three no-hitters, 12 one-hitters, 266 lifetime wins—in spite of the loss of four prime years to military service.

himself out of the lineup after playing in 2,130 consecutive games. His reflexes were gone, his coordination shot. Confused, bewildered, hurt, Gehrig asked the compassionate Joe McCarthy to take him out. Gehrig's illness was soon diagnosed as amyotrophic lateral sclerosis, a rare disease that attacks the central nervous system and leads to total incapacitation. In less than two years the Yankee Iron Man was dead, only thirty-eight years old.

DiMaggio and Feller were only two of the three all-time greats to enter baseball in the late thirties. The third was Theodore

Samuel Williams. One day in 1936 Red Sox general manager Eddie Collins went to the West Coast on a scouting trip. His purpose was to check out San Diego second baseman Bobby Doerr and another infielder. While he was there, he saw a lanky young left-handed hitting outfielder swing a bat. Collins's heart jumped. He bought Doerr, and for $35,000 he also bought Ted Williams, one of the greatest hitters who ever lived.

No hitter ever had more confidence at the plate than Ted Williams, every bit of it fully justified. No player ever had better eyesight, better judgment of a pitched ball, a purer swing, more power, more intense concentration. He lived to swing a bat, this tall, brash, fidgety youngster with the Hollywood good looks. He seemed to be never without a bat in his hands, be it on the field, in the dugout, in the clubhouse, and even in his hotel room, where one day an errant practice swing accidentally smashed a dresser mirror to pieces.

Ted Williams first came to spring training with the Red Sox in 1938. Still only nineteen, he was cocky, hard to discipline, and called his manager Joe Cronin "Sport." "Wait till you see Jimmie Foxx hit," someone said to him. And he answered, or so legend has it, "Wait till Foxx sees me hit." Nevertheless, he was farmed out to Minneapolis for seasoning. At that time the Red Sox had an all-.300-hitting outfield of Doc Cramer, Joe Vosmik, and Ben Chapman. "Tell 'em I'll be back," the departing Williams said, "and that I'm going to wind up making more money than the three of them put together."

He came back in 1939 and had an astonishing rookie season, batting .327, hitting 31 home runs, and leading the league with 145 runs batted in. He had an uncanny eye and rarely swung at a pitch that wasn't in the strike zone.

The first time he faced the Yankees, the New Yorkers held a meeting to discuss pitching to the new man. The consensus was right out of traditional wisdom: pitch him high and tight or low and away. The next day they held another meeting.

"Well," somebody asked, "what did we learn about Williams?"

Spud Chandler, who had pitched the day before, said, "I'll tell you what I learned. High and tight is ball one, and low and away is ball two." Williams wouldn't bite at anything an umpire would call a ball.

"Boys," catcher Bill Dickey said softly, with a shake of his head, "he's just a damned good hitter."

They would become the game's most stunning performers as the decade turned—DiMaggio, Feller, and Williams, symbols of the

Ted Williams. Six batting crowns, 521 home runs, lifetime batting average of .344—despite five seasons lost to military service in two wars.

Joe DiMaggio. Two home run titles, two batting crowns. Lifetime average: .325. Three years lost to military service.

American League's dominance. As ever, youth was moving aside the familiar names, setting new records, creating higher standards, fresh legends.

And something else happened in the waning days of the 1939 season. It was a quiet event, little noticed. A brief, two-paragraph story in the **New York Times** of August 27 reported that the doubleheader between the Dodgers and Reds at Ebbets Field had been played "before two prying electrical 'eyes.'" Major league baseball, the Times story went on, had "made its television debut." Television set owners "as far away as fifty miles viewed the action and heard the roar of the crowd."

Opening Day, April 16, 1940. A few hours after this picture was taken, twenty-one-year-old Bob Feller, **right**, pitched the only Opening Day no-hitter in baseball history. With Feller are Cleveland Manager Oscar Vitt, leaning on the bat, and catcher Rollie Hemsley.

Detroit's Bobo Newsom and Cincinnati's Paul Derringer exchange a less-than-hearty handshake before the seventh game of the 1940 World Series. Derringer outdueled Bobo to win it for the Reds.

War and Revolution
1940-1949

T HE annual Yankee pennant failed to materialize in 1940. The American League winner that year was Detroit, nosing out second-place Cleveland by one game and third-place New York by two.

The Tigers had a pair of .340 hitters in home run champ Hank Greenberg and young outfielder Barney McCosky. The power-hitting Rudy York was at first base, the flawless veteran Charlie Gehringer at second, Dick Bartell at shortstop, Pinky Higgins at third. The pitching staff included Schoolboy Rowe, Tommy Bridges, and the ace, the irrepressible Bobo Newsom, who logged a 21-5 won-lost record that season. Newsom's nickname stemmed from his habit of addressing everyone as Bobo—including, upon occasion, the saintly Connie Mack, whose closest friends addressed him respectfully as "Mr. Mack." In Bobo's defense, he changed teams so frequently that he could hardly be expected to remember everyone's name—in his 26-year career in organized baseball Bobo pitched for 18 different clubs.

Bob Feller launched his Cleveland team on opening day 1940 as no pitcher ever has before or since—with a no-hitter against the White Sox. In his fifth big league season, the twenty-one-year-old Feller won 27 games and led the league in earned run average, strikeouts, shutouts, innings pitched, and complete games.

Frank McCormick, Cincin-
nati's fine first baseman, who
led the National League in hits
in each of his first three
seasons in the big leagues.

It is April of 1941 and
Yankee rookie Phil Rizzuto,
hoping to make the team,
has been asked to pose with
the great DiMaggio.

In the National League in 1940 a pair of remarkable pitchers
hurled the Cincinnati Reds to their second pennant in a row. For
the second consecutive year converted infielder Bucky Walters and
Paul Derringer each won over 20 games. Despite the fact that they
featured only two solid hitters—Frank McCormick and Ernie
Lombardi—the Reds outlasted the Tigers to win the 1940 World
Series in seven games, Derringer beating a heroic Newsom 2-1 in
the finale. (Newsom's father died during the Series, and Bobo
wanted desperately to win the last game "for Dad.")

The last prewar season, 1941, was to provide some memorable
baseball history. One of the classic performances in all sports
began at Yankee Stadium on May 15, 1941. In that game Joe
DiMaggio singled once in four times at bat against the White Sox.

That innocuous single launched what was to become a tidal wave of excitement through the next two months. Day after day the Yankee Clipper continued to hit. On June 29 he hit in both games of a doubleheader in Washington, breaking George Sisler's American League record of hitting safely in 41 consecutive games.

DiMaggio's hitting streak gripped the imagination of baseball fans everywhere. In early July he broke Willie Keeler's 1897 major league record of 44 consecutive games. And he was just getting hot. From games 47 through 56 he came to bat 40 times and connected for 23 hits, a .575 average. Finally, on the night of July 17, in a game before over 60,000 fans in Cleveland, DiMaggio was stopped by pitchers Al Smith and Jim Bagby, Jr. But even then, it took two outstanding plays by Ken Keltner at third base to bring the streak to an end. DiMaggio had hit safely in 56 consecutive games, leaving the number "56" as one of baseball's most hallowed figures.

Stopping the great DiMaggio made the Cleveland management jubilant. The next day, however, when the ball park was less than half filled, they were crestfallen. Success had its penalties.

The last day of the 1941 season saw another remarkable under-pressure batting feat. Again, it was the spectacle of a great athlete responding brilliantly to a storybook challenge. Ted Williams, in his third year now, a bona fide star after seasons of batting .327 and .344, came down to the last day of the season facing a doubleheader against the Athletics and batting .39955—which rounded off to .400. Not since Harry Heilmann's .403 in 1923 had any American Leaguer achieved that most sublime of batting averages.

The night before, Red Sox manager Joe Cronin offered to keep Ted on the bench, out of the lineup, to preserve his .400 mark. However, Williams refused. His sense of pride and his idea of perfectionism would not allow it. "If I couldn't hit .400 all the way," he said later, "I didn't deserve it."

What Williams did that day exceeded all reasonable expectations. Swinging with lethal self-confidence, he got six hits in eight times at bat in the doubleheader and ended the season with a batting average of .406—a figure that has been shining over the baseball horizon ever since.

Despite Williams's superb hitting, and fine seasons by teammates Jimmie Foxx, Bobby Doerr, Joe Cronin, and Dominic DiMaggio, the Red Sox finished second in 1941, a distant 17 games behind the Yankees. New York featured the hitting of Joe DiMaggio, Tommy Henrich, Charlie Keller, Bill Dickey, Red Rolfe, and Joe Gordon, plus the sparkling play of rookie shortstop Phil Rizzuto.

Dominic DiMaggio of the Boston Red Sox. A star in his own right, Dom was always in the shadow of his brother Joe.

Vince DiMaggio, oldest of the three ball-playing DiMaggio brothers. A top-notch outfielder, Vince played for 10 years in the major leagues.

At bat: Number 5, Joltin' Joe DiMaggio. Hitting safely in his forty-fourth consecutive game, July 1, 1941.

Ken Keltner, Cleveland's long-time third baseman. Keltner is best remembered as the man whose brilliant fielding helped stop DiMaggio's 56-game hitting streak.

In the National League a rough-and-tumble 1941 Dodger team brought Brooklyn its first pennant since 1920, occasioning a borough-wide orgy of horn blowing, parading, partying, and pride. Led by the acid-tongued Leo Durocher, the Dodgers literally fought their way through a season of beanball wars, brawls, and umpire baiting to edge out a spirited Cardinal team by two and a half games. With Larry MacPhail running the front office and spending prodigal sums of money for players, the moribund, bankrupt Brooklyn franchise had been turned into one of the most exciting in baseball.

From the Phillies, MacPhail had bought slugging first baseman Dolph Camilli and pitcher Kirby Higbe; from the Cardinals, catcher Mickey Owen and outfielder Joe Medwick; from

Spud Chandler, owner of baseball's highest lifetime winning percentage: .717. Over eleven years of pitching for the Yankees he won 109 games and lost only 43.

Two of the American League's premier second basemen in the forties: Joe Gordon of the Yankees and Boston's Bobby Doerr.

the Cubs, stellar second baseman Billy Herman. The shrewd MacPhail had also picked up two American League castoffs, outfielder Dixie Walker and pitcher Whitlow Wyatt. Manager Leo Durocher's fine pitching staff was rounded out by veterans Curt Davis and Fred Fitzsimmons, and a sullen, hard-drinking relief pitcher, Hugh Casey.

In addition, the Dodgers had bought a baby-faced shortstop from the Red Sox organization, Pee Wee Reese, who would grow into the team's leader and one of the finest shortstops in National League history. And in center field they had one of the game's glittering jewels—a twenty-two-year-old "do-it-all" named Pete Reiser, one of the most naturally gifted ballplayers of all time.

Leo Durocher with the Cincinnati Reds in the early thirties. Leo gained fame as the aggressive manager of the Dodgers and the Giants in the forties and fifties. Previously he had been an equally aggressive short-stop with the Yankees, Reds, and Cardinals.

First baseman Dolph Camilli, the power man of the pennant-winning 1941 Dodgers. He led the National League in home runs and runs batted in that year and was voted the league's Most Valuable Player.

Joe Medwick.

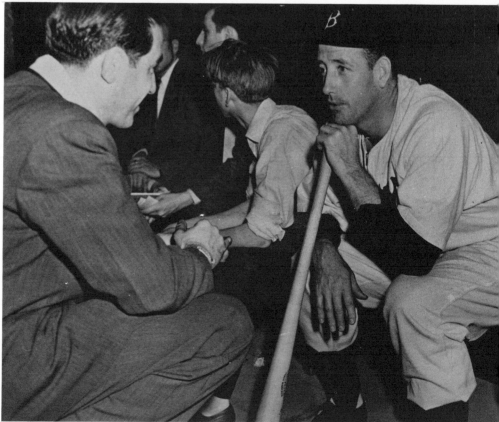

Joe Medwick stepping into one. The catcher is Clyde Sukeforth.

Shortstop Pee Wee Reese, **left**, and Joe Medwick, in 1941. (Also visible if you can find him: Dixie Walker.)

Whitlow Wyatt being interviewed before a game. Considered washed up in the American League, Wyatt joined the Dodgers in 1939. In 1941 he won 22 games, including a league-leading seven shutouts.

Pete Reiser in 1939.

Pete Reiser.

Pete Reiser being tagged out at home plate by Chicago's Bill Lee after trying to score from second on a wild pitch.

One of the darker moments in Brooklyn history: Mickey Owen has dropped the third strike, which should have ended the fourth game of the 1941 World Series. Tommy Henrich is about to break for first base, even as umpire Larry Goetz is calling him out.

Tommy Henrich in 1937. His clutch hitting
earned him the nickname "Old Reliable."

Phil Rizzuto, the Yankees' all-time shortstop.
He batted .307 in his rookie year, 1941, and was
voted the American League's Most Valuable
Player in 1950, when he batted .324.

Reiser could outrun anyone on a ball field; he could play both
the infield and outfield with consummate skill; he possessed a rifle
arm; he could hit from either side of the plate with slashing ferocity.
In 1941, his first full season, he led the National League with a
.343 batting average, leading also in doubles and triples. His future
seemed limitless. He was, however, doomed to suffer a series of
injuries that gradually drained his talent. Pistol Pete's relentless—
some said reckless—style of play often drove him into outfield
walls in pursuit of fly balls, resulting in numerous broken bones
and finally cutting short a career that was ultimately more notable
for its promise than its achievement.

The 1941 World Series was the first of many to be played
between the Yankees and Dodgers and, like most of those
encounters, provided baseball fans with an unforgettable moment.
In the '41 Series that moment occurred in the fourth game, at
Ebbets Field, in the top of the ninth inning. The Dodgers were

Johnny Allen, with the Brooklyn Dodgers in 1942. A tempestuous character, Allen had outstanding years with the Yankees and Indians in the thirties.

Elbie Fletcher, sharp-hitting, flashy-fielding first baseman for the Boston Braves and Pittsburgh Pirates.

Lou Novikoff of the Chicago Cubs. One of the most spectacular minor league hitters ever, the best he could do in the big leagues was one .300 season for the Cubs.

Phil Cavaretta, a steady and popular first baseman, spent 22 years in the big leagues, the first 20 with the Cubs. His best year was 1945, when he led the National League with a .355 batting average.

Sam Chapman, long-ball-
hitting outfielder for the
Athletics in the forties.

Johnny Mize, one of the mightiest sluggers in National League history.
In the thirties and forties he led the league in home runs four times
(with a high of 51 in 1947), in runs batted in three times, and in batting
average once. Later, in the fifties, he helped the Yankees win five
pennants and five World Championships.

Bucky Walters and his
manager, Bill McKechnie.

leading, 4-3, on the strength of a Pete Reiser home run, and
seemed about to deadlock the Series at two games apiece. What
took place in that top of the ninth was one of those things that
seemed to "happen only in Brooklyn."

Relief pitcher Hugh Casey had retired the first two Yankee
batters and gone to a full count of three balls and two strikes on
Yankee outfielder Tommy Henrich. Casey broke off a sharpbreak-
ing curve (some say it was a spitball), and Henrich swung and
missed—but the ball got away from Dodger catcher Mickey Owen
and Henrich reached first. What happened after that was pure
Yankee devastation. The infuriated Casey began fogging fastballs,
and the Yankees began hitting them. Joe DiMaggio singled. Charlie
Keller doubled home two runs. Bill Dickey walked. Joe Gordon
doubled home two more runs. The Yankees won, 7-4. They won
again the next day, ending Brooklyn's hopes for its first World
Championship.

By the time the 1942 season began, the country was at war. With the enactment of the first peacetime draft the year before, players had begun going into the service as early as 1941. Not long after Pearl Harbor, President Roosevelt wrote to Judge Landis: "I honestly feel that it would be best for the country to keep baseball going." It was Roosevelt's feeling that the game had a very positive and morale-building role to play in the troublesome years that lay ahead.

Baseball did carry on but not without difficulty. Before the start of the 1944 season, over 300 big league ballplayers (including most of the great names) were in the armed services, leaving behind patched-together ball clubs consisting of rejects and retreads, of bumbling youngsters and over-the-hill veterans like Paul Waner, who hung on because players were desperately needed. Cincinnati employed a fifteen-year-old pitcher, Joe Nuxhall, and in 1945 the St. Louis Browns fielded a man who came to symbolize the game's wartime patchwork quilt—the one-armed outfielder, Pete Gray.

Pete had lost his arm at the age of six. In the outfield, he caught the ball with his left (gloved) hand, placed the ball against his chest, let it roll out of his glove and up his wrist as he tucked the glove under the stub of his right arm, and then drew his left arm back across his chest until the ball rolled back into his hand. He was able to execute this maneuver so well that he could return the ball to the infield almost as quickly as an ordinary outfielder. Gray hit .333 for Memphis in the Southern Association in 1944, and in the outfield handled over 340 chances with only six errors. But American League pitching proved too much for him in 1945, and he batted only .218 in seventy-seven games.

To further dramatize the aberrations that prevailed during the war, 1944 saw the St. Louis Browns—the game's premier symbol of futility—win their first and only pennant (the solitude of this accomplishment was ensured a decade later when the Browns dissolved and reemerged as the Baltimore Orioles). The 1944 World Series was an all-St. Louis affair, as the Cardinals easily won their third straight pennant and then trounced the Browns in the World Series.

The Cardinals were led that season by one of wartime baseball's few legitimate talents, a youngster who had been converted from a sore-armed pitcher to an outfielder. He did not look very imposing up at the plate, with his slight build and his corkscrew batting stance, which someone said made him look "like a guilty kid peeking around a corner." Nevertheless, Stan Musial was to dominate National League hitting for years to come

Howie Pollet, longtime left-handed pitcher for the Cardinals. His best year was 1946, when he won 21 games and led the league in earned run average.

Harry "The Cat" Brecheen. He beat the Red Sox three times in the 1946 World Series.

Four Southpaws from St. Louis.

Max Lanier was six wins and no losses, and on his way to his best year, when he jumped to the Mexican League in 1946.

Ernie White. He pitched the game of his life in the 1942 World Series, shutting out the Yankees on six hits.

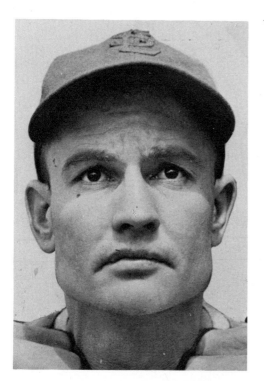

Walker Cooper.

One of the great brother batteries of all time, the Cooper brothers starred on the St. Louis pennant winners of 1942, '43, and '44. Walker was a hard-hitting catcher, and Mort won over 20 games in each of those seasons.

Mort Cooper.

Johnny Beazley had one brilliant year for the Cardinals, 1942, when he won 21 games and went on to beat the Yankees twice in the World Series. Unfortunately, he suffered an arm injury while in military service and lost his effectiveness.

Enos Slaughter, a nonstop hustler for all of his 19 big league seasons. He was a fine outfielder and a strong hitter. His best season was 1949 when he hit .336. He had 10 seasons of over .300 and finished his 19 years with exactly that batting average.

Stanley Frank Musial in 1943.

Before his long career came to a close in 1963, Musial had established a host of National League records. The Donora, Pennsylvania, native led the league in batting seven times, in hits six times, in doubles seven times, and triples five times, in addition to countless other feats. Voted the league's Most Valuable Player in 1943, '46, and '48, he was the most engaging and congenial of great stars. Seemingly without temperament or ego, he went about his business, day in and day out, drilling line drives, winning ball games, never complaining, always smiling. One day before a game, a sportswriter sat down next to Stan the Man on the bench and jokingly asked him why he seemed to always be smiling. "Well,"

→

Nicknamed "The Octopus," Marty Marion starred at shortstop for four St. Louis pennant winners in the forties.

Fifteen-year-old Joe Nuxhall in his high school uniform in 1944. A few weeks later he was signed by Cincinnati and became the youngest player ever to play in the major leagues. He pitched two-thirds of an inning for Cincinnati on June 10, 1944, when he was 15 years, 10 months, and 11 days old, and left with a 67.50 earned run average. He came back to the big leagues in 1952, however, and remained for 15 years, winning 135 games.

answered Musial, who at that time was batting in the .360s, commanded a huge salary, and was universally admired, "if you were me, wouldn't you be smiling?"

There was one man, during the war years, who was looking ahead: Branch Rickey. Rickey, who had built the fine Cardinal teams that ruled the National League in the early forties, had become general manager of the Dodgers late in 1942, after Larry MacPhail's resignation to accept a commission in the army.

As he had done in St. Louis, Rickey had his scouts scattered across the land signing any youth who showed even the merest glimmer of talent. No matter that most of them would not be packaged for delivery until after the war; the war would be over in due time, and when it was Rickey would be ahead of everybody else. Among those caught in the vast Rickey net were youngsters named Carl Erskine, Duke Snider, and Gil Hodges.

But this time Rickey's planning went deeper. By the fall of 1945 the war was over, and now the revolution was about to begin.

Baseball, the wholesome game of summer, the fantasy world of millions of youngsters, America's National Pastime, had long been a national disgrace. Since the 1880s, organized baseball had banned from its ranks some of the finest players in the country for the quaint reason that their skin was the wrong color.

There had developed through the years a "gentlemen's agreement" between the club owners to keep the national game lily white—this in spite of the abilities shown by black players in their own loosely organized leagues and in postseason games against teams of big leaguers. In the Negro leagues, the pay was poor, travel

Pete Gray, the one-armed outfielder. He appeared in 77 games for the St. Louis Browns in 1945 and batted .218.

The only pennant-winning infield in the St. Louis Browns' history. **Left to right:** reserve infielder Ellis Clary, shortstop Vern Stephens, reserve infielder Floyd Baker, third baseman Mark Christman, second baseman Don Gutteridge, and first baseman George McQuinn.

Vern Stephens, home-run-hitting shortstop for the Browns and Red Sox in the forties. He hit 39 home runs in 1949 and drove in 159 runs.

The only pennant-winning pitching staff in the St. Louis Browns' history. **Left to right:** Nelson Potter, Denny Galehouse, Jack Kramer, Bob Muncrief, and Sigmund Jakucki.

conditions intolerable, and recognition virtually nonexistent. (John McGraw, whose flinty soul melted at the sight of talent, twice tried to slip blacks onto the Giants, passing one off as a Cuban and the other as an Indian, but he did not get away with it.)

Decade after decade saw the brilliant talents of such blacks as Cyclone Joe Williams, Cannonball Dick Redding, John Henry Lloyd, Cool Papa Bell, Oscar Charleston, Martin Dihago, Buck Leonard, Josh Gibson, Satchel Paige, and countless others wasted in the shadows and back alleys of baseball because of bigotry and injustice. If it were not for Branch Rickey, the list might well have been extended to include Willie Mays, Henry Aaron, Roberto Clemente, Frank Robinson, Bob Gibson, Ernie Banks, Lou Brock, Rod Carew—and, of course, Jackie Robinson.

On October 23, 1945, Rickey announced that the Brooklyn Dodgers had signed to a Montreal (International League) contract two Negroes, Jackie Robinson, shortstop for the black Kansas City Monarchs, and Johnny Wright, pitcher for the Newark Eagles.

The Cardinals putting on the "Williams Shift" in the 1946 World Series at Sportsman's Park in St. Louis. As Ted Williams waits at the plate, pitcher Howie Pollet watches his defense realign itself. Center field is completely deserted.

Enos Slaughter's most famous moment. With the score tied in the bottom of the eighth inning of the seventh game of the 1946 World Series, Slaughter scores from first on a looping single by Harry Walker. Red Sox shortstop Johnny Pesky's split-second delay in getting the relay home enabled Slaughter to make it.

Fred Hutchinson, a greatly admired pitcher for the Detroit Tigers in the forties. Later, he managed the Tigers, Cardinals, and Reds.

Jackie Robinson and Branch Rickey.

James "Cool Papa" Bell, one of the Negro Leagues' great players of the 1920s and 1930s. His defensive abilities in the outfield and his speed on the bases were legendary.

From the beginning it was obvious that Robinson was the man Rickey had zeroed in on (Wright soon disappeared from the scene).

Jack Roosevelt Robinson was the man Rickey wanted and the man that baseball—in spite of itself—needed. Rickey wanted more than just playing ability—which he knew Robinson had in abundance. He also had to have a man of intelligence, courage, and a sense of destiny. All of these Robinson also had in abundance.

From the beginning, nothing came easy for Jackie Robinson. With restrictive racial laws still rampant in the postwar South, Robinson could not eat in the same restaurants as his teammates, nor stay at the same hotels. In some towns there were local ordinances forbidding him to play on the same field with whites. And when he did play, there were vicious racial catcalls, beanballs, and attempted spikings. There was resentment from teammates, Southerners and Northerners both. Some teammates asked to be traded rather than play alongside Robinson, and these Rickey would accommodate (but only when the deal was to the advantage of the Dodgers). Others, however, like Pee Wee Reese and Eddie Stanky, openly demonstrated their support of Robinson.

Josh Gibson.

Josh Gibson—who was called The Jimmie Foxx of the Negro Leagues—never had a chance to play in the major leagues.

DODGERS CLUB HOUSE

KEEP OUT

Jackie Robinson.

Jackie Robinson trying to steal home. The batter is Billy Cox. (Jackie successfully stole home 20 times in his career.)

Monte Irvin, left, and Larry Doby, of the
Negro Leagues' Newark Eagles, shortly
before they entered organized ball.

Satchel Paige, greatest pitcher in the
history of the Negro Leagues. He finally
got his chance in the big leagues in
1948 with Bill Veeck's Cleveland
Indians.

Eddie Stanky—brash, aggressive, intelligent—was second baseman for three different pennant winners: the 1947 Dodgers, the 1948 Braves, and the 1951 Giants.

Pitcher Max Lanier with Vera Cruz in the Mexican League in 1946.

Ewell Blackwell of the Cincinnati Reds. During 1947 he won 16 straight games. Included in his streak were a no-hitter against the Braves and a near second consecutive no-hitter against the Dodgers—broken up by a ground ball single in the ninth inning by Eddie Stanky (which Blackwell himself just missed picking up).

Mickey Vernon won the American League batting title in 1946 with a .353 batting average, and again in 1953 with .337.

Eddie Miksis, pinch-running for Pete Reiser, scoring the winning run on Cookie Lavagetto's double in the bottom of the ninth inning in the fourth game of the 1947 World Series (breaking up Bevens's no-hitter). The Yankees' catcher is Yogi Berra.

Tex Hughson was a 20-game winner for the Red Sox in 1942 and again in 1946.

Hugh Casey, **left**, winning Brooklyn pitcher in the fourth game, and pinch-hitting hero Cookie Lavagetto.

Brooklyn outfielder Al Gionfriddo has just made his spectacular catch
of Joe DiMaggio's bid for a three-run, game-tying home run in the
sixth game of the 1947 World Series, at Yankee Stadium.

Bobby Bragan, slick-fielding catcher for the Phillies and Dodgers in the forties. Bragan later had a distinguished managerial career.

Rickey had placed upon Robinson one iron-bound, inflexible, restriction: there must be no incidents. Robinson must not fight back. The "cause," Rickey stressed over and over, was all-important, more important than Robinson, more important than any single individual. To prove this, Rickey passed up signing another black player of outstanding talent, Larry Doby, because he heard that Cleveland was interested in Doby. In 1947 Doby became the second black to play in the major leagues, and the first in the American League. The "cause" was expanding. But ever so slowly. The Yankees, for instance, did not field their first black player until Elston Howard in 1955; and Boston's Tom Yawkey, who through the years spent millions of dollars trying to buy a pennant, did not have a black on the Red Sox until 1959.

Jackie Robinson joined the Dodgers in 1947 and sparked them to a pennant, running the bases with breathless daring. (Over his career he stole home 20 times.) Once his teammates saw he could help put money in their pockets, he gradually won acceptance. A key episode occurred early in the 1947 season. On the Dodgers' first trip into St. Louis there were rumors that the Cardinals would go on strike rather than appear on the same field with him. Into this simmering situation stepped the president of the National League, Ford Frick. Never a man for strong

Five members of the 1946 Dodgers, who finished the season in a tie with the Cardinals. Hugh Casey is at the top; the others, **left to right**: Pete Reiser, Cookie Lavagetto, Pee Wee Reese, and Dixie Walker.

Johnny Sain, ace right-hander of the Boston Braves in the 1940s. Sain was a four-time 20-game winner for the Braves, with 24 victories in the pennant-winning year 1948.

Outfielder-third base-man Sid Gordon of the Giants, a favorite of New York fans in the forties.

Player-manager Lou Boudreau led the Cleveland Indians to an American League pennant and a World Championship in 1948. He batted .355 and was voted the league's Most Valuable Player. The 1948 season ended with Cleveland and Boston tied for first place; in a one-game play-off on October 4, Boudreau hit two home runs and the Indians won, 8-3, to take the American League pennant. Cleveland then went on to beat the Boston Braves in the World Series, four games to two.

Bobo Newsom. One of the most traveled of all ballplayers, Bobo played for 18 different teams during his long career, nine in the majors and nine in the minors. Once he decided to experimentally find out Joe DiMaggio's weakness, and he threw him a different pitch every time DiMaggio came to bat. Joltin' Joe hit a homer, a couple of triples, and a double. "I've got it." said Bobo. "His weakness is two-base hits."

Bob Feller.

statements, Frick, to his eternal credit, met the challenge with full
force, issuing a ringing declaration that read:

> "I do not care if half the league strikes. Those who do it will
> encounter quick retribution. All will be suspended and I do not
> care if it wrecks the National League for five years. This is the
> United States of America and one citizen has as much right to
> play as another."

As time passed and Robinson gradually became accepted, and Rickey's restrictions became less important, the "real" Robinson emerged. This was a fiery, dynamic, abrasively outspoken man; a fighter, a battler, a militant. When one remembers this uncompromising and competitive crusader, one can only look back upon his early years of disciplined forebearance with amazement at his self-control.

Robinson was not the only story in that postwar year of 1946. Other vibrations were coming from south of the border, where the impossibly wealthy Pasquel brothers, notably Jorge, began luring major leaguers to Mexico with large sums of money in an attempt to build a Mexican League. A number of players went chasing after Mexican gold, most prominent among them the Cardinals' fine left-hander Max Lanier, Brooklyn catcher Mickey Owen, and a handful of others, including the then little-known Giant right-hander Sal Maglie. Others, including Stan Musial, Ted Williams, and Pete Reiser resisted the Pasquels' blandishments.

Commissioner Albert Benjamin "Happy" Chandler, a Kentucky politician who had been elected to the position upon the death of Judge Landis in 1944, immediately slapped five-year suspensions on the departed players. The Mexican League soon collapsed, however, leaving some of the players holding empty financial bags. Those who returned to the United States eventually won reinstatement in 1949.

After losing the 1946 National League pennant to the St. Louis Cardinals in an unprecedented play-off necessitated by a tie, the Dodgers won the flag in 1947 and went into a second World Series against the Yankees. The '47 Series is remembered for two

Roy Sievers played in the big leagues for 17 years, from 1949 through 1965, mostly with the Browns and Senators. In 1957 he led the American League in home runs and runs batted in.

The heart of Detroit's lineup in 1949. **Left to right:** third baseman George Kell, left fielder Hoot Evers, right fielder Vic Wertz, and center fielder Johnny Groth.

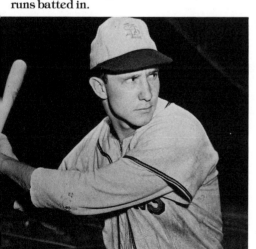

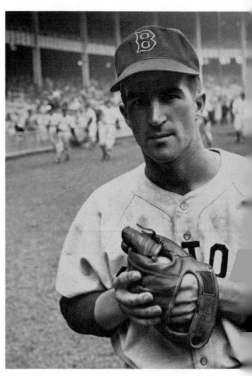

Mel Parnell, one of the best left-handers ever to pitch for the Boston Red Sox.

Johnny Pesky, shortstop for the Red Sox, led the American League in hits his first three years in the big leagues (1942, 1946, and 1947).

outstanding moments. In the sixth game, Brooklyn left-fielder Al Gionfriddo made a spectacular catch of Joe DiMaggio's bid for a three-run home run, giving the Dodgers a victory and forcing the Series into a seventh game—which the Yankees won. (Ironically, Gionfriddo was sent back to the minors the next year and never played another game in the major leagues.)

But the highlight of the 1947 Series, and in fact one of the storybook moments in all of sports history, occurred in the fourth game, at Ebbets Field. Going into the bottom of the ninth inning the Yankees were ahead, 2-1, with Floyd Bevens pitching a **no-hitter** for New York—albeit a ragged one, having allowed eight walks. With an unassisted triple play and Mickey Owen's dropped third strike already part of their World Series experience, Dodger fans were wondering if now they were to be subjected to the humiliation of a World Series no-hitter.

Bevens, hitherto a pitcher of minor distinction, now stood at the brink of baseball immortality. No one had ever pitched a World Series no-hitter. He retired the first Brooklyn batter in the ninth inning on a fly ball to DiMaggio. Carl Furillo drew Bevens's ninth walk. The next batter fouled out to Yankee first baseman George

Ralph Kiner.

Joe DiMaggio.

Joe Page, superb relief
pitcher for the Yankees
in the late 1940s, leaning
on the bullpen rail at
Yankee Stadium.

McQuinn. Two were out and only one more needed for a no-hitter.

At this point Al Gionfriddo was put in to run for Furillo and an
injured Pete Reiser sent up to hit for Brooklyn pitcher Hugh Casey.
Gionfriddo promptly stole second. Yankee manager Bucky Harris
then defied the baseball gods by putting the winning run on base—
ordering Reiser walked. Underlining this unorthodox move even
more was the fact that Reiser had a fractured ankle and could barely
run. "He can still swing," Harris said. Eddie Miksis ran for Reiser.
Now there were two men on base and two outs. Still, only one more
out needed for Bevens's no-hitter.

Joe Page taking on another
assignment at Yankee
Stadium on September 13,
1949. Casey Stengel is
holding the ball. The
outgoing pitcher is Clarence
"Cuddles" Marshall. The
catcher is Yogi Berra.

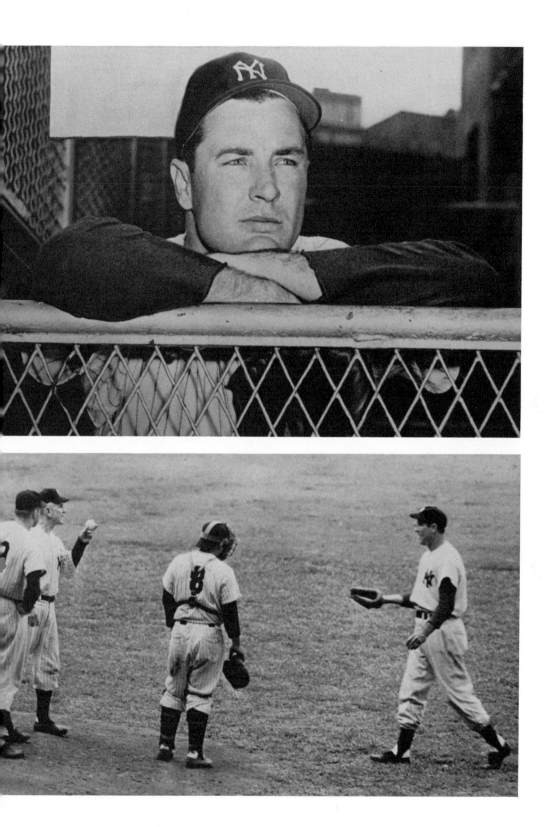

Uncharacteristically, Stan Musial has just popped up. Bruce Edwards
is the catcher.

Eddie Stanky was the next Brooklyn batter, but veteran third baseman Harry "Cookie" Lavagetto was sent up to pinch-hit. Lavagetto, at the end of his career now, but a renowned clutch hitter, promptly lined a double off the right-field wall—scoring both runners and depriving Bevens not only of a no-hitter but of a victory as well. (Strangely, like Gionfriddo, neither Lavagetto nor Bevens ever played another game in the major leagues.)

In July of 1948 the Dodgers and Giants were engaged in the most startling managerial switch in baseball history. At the time Leo Durocher was managing the Dodgers while Brooklyn's deadly crosstown adversary, the Giants, were being managed by one of the club's all-time heroes, the likable, mild-mannered Mel Ott, subject of Durocher's famous but fallacious dictum, "Nice guys finish last." While reluctant to fire Ott, Giants owner Horace Stoneham had been anxious to make a change for some time. Meanwhile, in Brooklyn, Rickey had become disenchanted with the brilliant but unpredictable Durocher. A meeting was arranged between Rickey and Stoneham, the result of which was Ott's "promotion" to a front-office job while Durocher moved from the Dodgers to the Giants, a move that left many Dodger fans bemused and many Giant fans outraged—the man they had for so many years loved to hate was now leading their team.

While Ted Williams and Joe DiMaggio continued to dominate hitting in the American League in the latter part of the decade, and Stan the Man Musial continued his systematic torture of National League pitchers, a young powerhouse with the lowly Pittsburgh Pirates was year by year engraving his name among the greatest of all home run hitters. Beginning with his first year, 1946, Ralph Kiner was to lead or tie for the National League lead in home runs for seven consecutive years, something not even the mighty Ruth had been able to do. Twice Kiner passed the fifty mark, with 51 home runs in 1947 and 54 in 1949. Although his lifetime home run total of 369 is far down on the list of all-time leaders, Kiner, who played only ten seasons in the big leagues, ranks among the foremost home run hitters in baseball history. Over his career he homered on average once every 14.1 times at bat, a pace exceeded only by Babe Ruth (who homered on average once every 11.8 times at bat).

In 1949 the Dodgers and Yankees again met in the World Series. It turned out to be, for them, a comparatively uneventful meeting, with the Yankees winning in five games. Both clubs had won their pennants on the last day of the season, the Dodgers in 10 innings over Philadelphia, the Yankees beating the Red Sox.

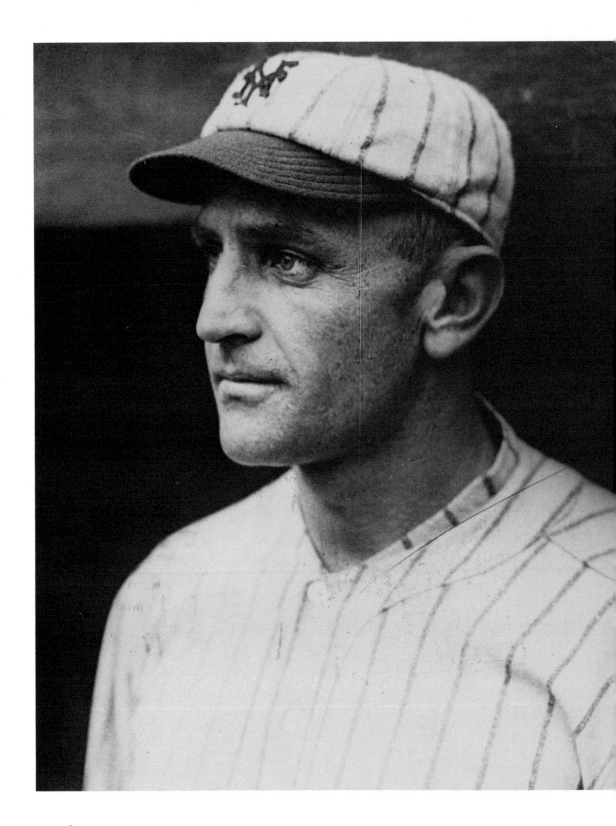

Manager Casey Stengel in the Yankee dugout in 1949. Next to him is Joe Page.

←

Casey Stengel as an outfielder with John McGraw's Giants in the early twenties.

For the Yankees, it was the beginning of an incredible string of 14 pennants in 16 years, the first 10 of which were won under their new manager, a craggy-faced baseball veteran named Casey Stengel. Before he took over the Yankees, Stengel, a prominent managerial failure with both the Brooklyn Dodgers and the Boston Braves, and a man who talked in clouds of verbiage that seemed to have no logic, had been known as a character and a clown. By the time he left the Yankees, after the 1960 season, he was still known as a character and a clown, but now the word **genius** had been added as well. No one has ever matched his record of five straight World Championships (1949 through 1953).

Ted Williams.

The Boston Red Sox, fielding baseball's mightiest offensive team, had been denied two years in a row by the narrowest of margins; in 1948 in a one-game play-off with Cleveland, and in 1949 losing on the last day of the season to the Yankees. Led by Ted Williams, the Boston lineup featured hitters like Vern Stephens, Bobby Doerr, Dom DiMaggio, Johnny Pesky, and Billy Goodman. But in 1948 they lost to a Cleveland team led and inspired by player-manager Lou Boudreau, and in 1949 to an injury-ridden Yankee team skillfully manipulated by Stengel. Stengel's magnificent trio of pitchers—Raschi, Reynolds, and Lopat—were anchored by a fastballing relief pitcher name Joe Page.

The Dodger ball club of 1949 now contained the nucleus of the team that was to ravage the National League for the first half of the next decade. Stocked with right-handed power to take advantage of Ebbets Field's short left-field wall, the Dodgers had Gil Hodges at first base, Jackie Robinson at second, Pee Wee Reese at short, and a defensive genius, Billy Cox, at third. Duke Snider and Carl Furillo were the outfield regulars, with Roy Campanella behind the plate. Brooklyn's pitching was topped by Don Newcombe, Preacher Roe, Ralph Branca, and Carl Erskine.

In 1949, Jackie Robinson was voted the league's Most Valuable Player; he was its leading hitter, batting .342, and its number-one base-stealer. Nevertheless, in 1949, four years after his entry into professional baseball, Robinson was one of only five blacks to appear in National League games. The others were his teammates Newcombe and Campanella, and infielder Henry Thompson and outfielder Monte Irvin of the Giants. In the American League, in 1949, there were onlys two blacks, Larry Doby and Satchel Paige, both with Bill Veeck's Cleveland Indians.

Three clubs out of 16 had seen the future and believed it.

Robin Roberts.

A Miracle, the Yankees, and Westward Ho

1950-1959

WHILE the Yankees opened the decade in high style in 1950, winning the second of their five consecutive American League pennants and World Championships, the Dodgers ran into a spirited band of Philadelphians known as "The Whiz Kids." The Whiz Kids were actually a combination of young and old, the young being shortstop Granny Hamner, third baseman Willie Jones, outfielders Del Ennis and Richie Ashburn, and a pair of scintillating pitching stars, Robin Roberts and Curt Simmons. The "old" were first baseman Eddie Waitkus, second baseman Mike Goliat, catcher Andy Seminick (each of them all of thirty), and a thirty-three-year-old relief pitcher named Jim Konstanty whose work was so outstanding that year it earned him the league's Most Valuable Player honors.

The surprising Phillies seemed to have it locked up going into the final weeks of the 1950 season; but then, with a pitching staff suddenly riddled with injuries to starters Bob Miller and Bubba Church, and with ace left-hander Simmons called to active military duty on September 10, the Phillies began a precarious slide— toward the waiting arms of the Dodgers.

Curt Simmons.

The Whiz Kids' inner defense in 1950. **Left to right:** catcher Andy Seminick, third baseman Willie Jones, shortstop Granny Hamner, second baseman Mike Goliat, and first baseman Eddie Waitkus.

Richie Ashburn, center fielder for the 1950 Phillies. Ashburn won batting titles in 1955 and 1958 with averages of .338 and .350.

Roy Campanella tagging Ferris Fain at home plate in the 1951 All-Star game at Detroit.

Warren Spahn.

Sal Maglie, nicknamed The
Barber for the close shaves
he gave to hitters. He won
23 games for the Giants in
1951.

Alvin Dark, shortstop for the 1951 Miracle
Giants. Rookie of the Year with the Braves in
1948, Dark was traded with Eddie Stanky to the
Giants after the 1949 season.

Willie Mays.

Polo Grounds, October 3, 1951. The Miracle is only several seconds old. Brooklyn pitcher Ralph Branca, his name freshly emblazoned upon baseball lore, is leaving the mound. Jackie Robinson is in the foreground. Bobby Thomson (unseen) is still circling the bases.

Bobby Thomson has arrived.

The Whiz Kids came into Ebbets Field at the end of the season with a two-game lead and two to play. On Saturday afternoon the Dodgers won. Another Dodger win the following day would bring a tie and a play-off. The game on Sunday afternoon, before a packed house at Ebbets Field, developed into a sizzling pitching duel between two splendid young fireballers, Robin Roberts and Don Newcombe. With the score tied, 1-1, in the bottom of the ninth inning, the Dodgers almost won it: with men on first and second, Duke Snider lined a single to center; Dodger Cal Abrams, however, was thrown out at the plate by Richie Ashburn. The Dodgers then loaded the bases with one out but, pitching with the grit that was so typical of him, Robin Roberts survived by retiring Carl Furillo

It is still October 3, 1951. An inconsolable Ralph Branca is in the Brooklyn dressing room after the game. (For those who find significance in such things, Branca wore uniform number 13.)

The year 1951 and a changing of the guard: Joe DiMaggio's last year, young Mickey Mantle's first.

Mickey Mantle.

Yogi Berra.

and Gil Hodges. In the top of the tenth, the Phillies' Dick Sisler—son of the great George Sisler—ended the agony by lining a Newcombe pitch into the left-field seats with two men on. The final score was 4-1, and the Phillies were the National League champions for the first time since 1915.

It was the last time the Phillies would win that year. In the 1950 World Series the Yankees beat them four straight. Stengel's four starters in that Series were, in order, Vic Raschi, Allie Reynolds, Eddie Lopat, and Whitey Ford, surely the four best pitchers ever to start in a single Series for one team. The four-game sweep was the seventh in World Series history—once by the 1914 Braves, the other six times by Yankee teams.

Gerry Coleman played a sparkling second base for the Yankees. He was especially adept as an acrobatic pivot man in executing double plays. (Here the victim, out at second, is outfielder Jerry Scala of the White Sox.) Coleman was voted the Most Valuable Player in the 1950 World Series and hit .364 in the 1957 Series.

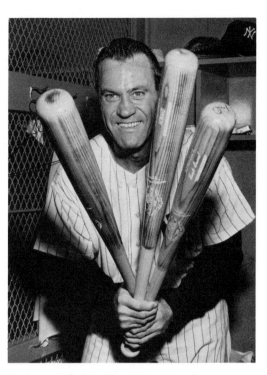

Vic Raschi, Casey Stengel's clutch pitcher in 1949. Three times a 20-game winner, Raschi won the biggest game of his life when he beat the Red Sox on the last day of the 1949 season to clinch the pennant.

Yankee outfielder Hank Bauer hit four home runs against Milwaukee in the 1958 World Series.

Eddie Lopat, one of Stengel's pitching stalwarts on the 1949 through 1953 World Champion Yankees.

Allie Reynolds, Yankee fireballer, pitched two no-hit games in 1951.

The only major league appearance of a "player" who is today more famous than many a .300 hitter. In order to stimulate attendance, St. Louis Browns' owner Bill Veeck signed a twenty-six-year-old midget, Eddie Gaedel, to a contract. Gaedel came to bat as a pinch hitter at Sportsman's Park in St. Louis against the Tigers on August 19, 1951. Tiger pitcher Bob Cain walked him on four pitches—all high. Gaedel then left the game for a pinch runner. The next day Veeck received a telegram from American League president Will Harridge condemning such "stunts," and Gaedel never played again. Gaedel was 3 feet 7 inches and weighed 65 pounds. The catcher is Bob Swift, the umpire Ed Hurley.

It is the seventh game of the 1952 World Series against the Dodgers and Casey Stengel is giving the word to his players. They listened. The Yankees won.

Al Rosen, Cleveland's rugged third baseman. Rosen's finest year was 1953 when he batted .336 and led the league with 43 home runs and 145 runs batted in. He was voted the league's Most Valuable Player that year.

Bobby Avila, Mexican-born second baseman on Cleveland's pennant winner in 1954. He led the league in batting that year with a .341 average.

The front four of perhaps the greatest pitching staff ever. **Left to right:** Mike Garcia, Early Wynn, Bob Feller, and Bob Lemon.

Outfielder Jackie Jensen. He came up with the Yankees but had his finest seasons with the Red Sox. Jensen was the American League leader in runs batted in three times.

The man who had pitched the Phillies into the World Series for only the second time in their history was destined to become one of baseball's great pitchers. Robin Roberts's talent was immediately apparent to all who saw him. When he showed up one afternoon in the summer of 1947 to demonstrate his abilities for the Phillies, one of their coaches, a shrewd old catcher named Cy Perkins, watched the youngster throw a few pitches and immediately said to some front-office personnel, "Don't let that kid out of the park."

In an age of large bonuses, the Phillies signed Roberts for the discount price of $25,000 (teammate Curt Simmons reportedly received $65,000). He was a tireless worker, throwing a low, rising fastball with excellent control. Roberts possessed the uncanny ability—all great athletes do—to find new reservoirs of strength when necessary. In the late innings of a close game, opposing batters swore, his fastball started moving better than it had in the early innings. His concentration on the mound was so total that often he would say to a teammate after a game, "Was there a big crowd out there today?"

In 1950 Roberts began a string of six consecutive seasons of 20 or more victories, reaching his peak in 1952 with a record of 28 wins and 7 losses.

Dusty Rhodes, pinch-hitting hero of the Giants' four-game 1954 World Series sweep of the Cleveland Indians.

Johnny Antonelli. The Braves paid him a large bonus, then dealt him to the Giants for whom he won 21 games in 1954.

Willie Mays about to catch Vic Wertz's 460-foot drive to deep center field in the eighth inning of the opening game of the 1954 World Series. At the time, the score was tied and two Indians were on base.

Herb Score.

Ferris Fain won back-to-back American League batting titles in 1951 and 1952, with averages of .344 and .327.

Having made the catch, Mays is wheeling around and throwing the ball back to the infield. Everything was done in one motion. Instead of two men scoring, none did, and the Giants went on to win the game in the tenth inning.

Manager Chuck Dressen and four key members of his 1952 National League pennant winners. **Back row:** Joe Black, **left,** and Pee Wee Reese. **Front:** Duke Snider, **left,** Dressen, and Jackie Robinson. Black pitched extraordinary relief ball for Brooklyn that year.

Clem Labine, Brooklyn's superb sinker-ball-throwing relief specialist.

Jackie Robinson.

Billy Cox. No better defensive
third baseman ever lived.

Gil Hodges is safe at home. The place is Ebbets Field in April 1951. The catcher is Philadelphia's Andy Seminick.

Carl Erskine, 20-game winner for the Dodgers in 1953. Erskine pitched no-hit games in 1952 and 1956. In the 1953 World Series he set a record—since broken—when he struck out 14 Yankees in one game.

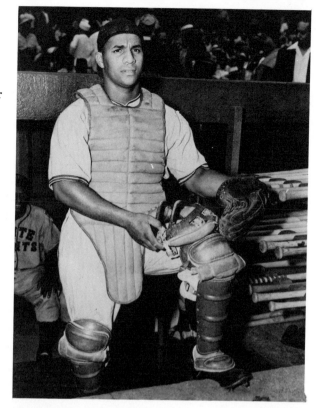

Roy Campanella as the catcher of the Baltimore Elite Giants in the Negro Leagues in 1945. Playing for Brooklyn, Campanella was the National League's Most Valuable Player in 1951, 1953, and 1955.

Roy Campanella has just tagged the Yankees' Billy Martin out at the plate in the fourth game of the 1953 World Series. It was the final out of the game.

Dodger shortstop Pee Wee Reese.

Duke Snider, Brooklyn's answer to Mays and Mantle. A sparkling center fielder, Snider had five consecutive years of 40 or more home runs. Duke hit four home runs in the 1952 World Series and again in 1955.

Don Newcombe, Brooklyn's fastballing right-hander. Three times a 20-game winner, Newcombe's finest year was 1956, when he won 27 and lost 7. He was voted the National League's Most Valuable Player that year.

The National League's other premier pitcher in the 1950s was a tireless left-hander with the Braves named Warren Spahn. What Dean and Hubbell were to the league in the thirties, Roberts and Spahn were in the fifties. A story told about Spahn has him warming up one day with veteran catcher Ernie Lombardi. The year is 1942 and Spahn is a twenty-one-year-old rookie proud of his fastball. Spahn throws one of his blazers wide of the mark. The powerful, ham-handed Lombardi does not shift his feet but instead sticks out his bare hand and plucks the ball out of the air. The young Spahn might have been chagrined, but the great pitcher-to-be inside of him realized at that moment that he was going to need more than a fastball to get by in this man's league. And so he developed an arsenal of pitches—sliders, screwballs, curves, change-ups—all of which he learned to deliver with pinpoint control.

Spahn did not win his first major league game until after his return from military service in 1946, at the age of twenty-five. But once he began winning, he simply did not stop. No pitcher in modern times has been more consistent. Blessed with an arm seemingly immune from injury or fatigue, between 1947 and 1963 he never started less than 32 games nor more than 39. Thirteen times he won 20 or more games in a season, something achieved only by the mighty Mathewson. At the age of 42, in 1963, he won 23 games and lost only 7. His 363 lifetime wins stands fifth on the all-time list, topped only by the Valhalla names of Cy Young, Walter Johnson, Christy Mathewson, and Grover Cleveland Alexander.

When he took over the Giants in 1948, Leo Durocher said to owner Horace Stoneham, "Give me my kind of team and we'll win." Gradually a powerhouse team that had been a chronic loser was dismantled. Traded away were such heavy-hitting but slow-footed stars as Johnny Mize, Walker Cooper, Willard Marshall, and Sid Gordon. By 1951 Durocher had his team in place. It included the scrappy Eddie Stanky, skillful bat manipulators like Whitey Lockman, Alvin Dark, Don Mueller, hard hitters like Monte Irvin and Henry Thompson, and a pitching staff led by three fine starters, Sal Maglie, Larry Jansen, and Jim Hearn.

Durocher's team stumbled badly in the spring of 1951, with a losing streak of 11 games. Meanwhile, the strong Brooklyn team was sprinting. On August 11 the Dodgers' lead was 13½ games. What happened then has been a rallying cry for second-place teams ever since. The Giants tore off a winning streak of 16, won 39 of their last 47 games, and ended the season in a tie with the Dodgers.

Thus for the second time in six seasons the Dodgers found themselves in a tie requiring a three-game play-off for the pennant (the first time had been the tie with the Cardinals in 1946). The first two games were divided, the Giants winning the first, the Dodgers the second. Then the two teams got set to play the crowning game of the 1951 season, on October 3, 1951.

What happened that afternoon at the Polo Grounds may someday be equaled for drama but will surely never be topped. With a tired Don Newcombe pitching gallantly, the Dodgers took a 4-1 lead into the bottom of the ninth inning, having routed a season-long tormentor, curve-baller Sal Maglie. Coming to bat with that same spirit of resolution that had characterized them down the homestretch, the Giants led off with singles by Alvin Dark and Don Mueller. The potential tying run came to the plate in the person of the Giants' top hitter, Monte Irvin. Newcombe got him to pop to Gil Hodges in foul ground. Whitey Lockman then slapped an opposite-field double to left, making the score 4-2 and putting men on second and third.

At this point Dodger manager Charlie Dressen removed Don Newcombe and brought in right-hander Ralph Branca, who through the years had been an effective, sometimes brilliant, pitcher for the Dodgers. The Giants' batter was Bobby Thomson, a right-handed swinger of considerable ability who had never quite fulfilled his early promise. But whatever Thomson had or had not done in the past, whatever he would or would not do in the future, would be of little consequence as far as the baseball world was concerned. For it was at that moment, on October 3, 1951, at the Polo Grounds, that the name of Bobby Thomson would be etched and associated forever with a swing of the bat so stunning and incredible as to make believers of dreamers everywhere.

Branca threw two pitches. The first was a strike. The second? That one is still going, and will continue to go as long as baseball is played. It made the score New York 5, Brooklyn 4, and the Giants, not the Dodgers, the champions of the National League.

The Miracle Giants of 1951 were by and large a team of experienced players. Their generating force, however, was a twenty-year-old center fielder named Willie Howard Mays. On May 25 the Giants called Mays up from their Minneapolis farm club in the American Association where he was hitting a rather noticeable .477.

Not only did Mays play superbly—he hit with power and for average, he ran well, he threw and fielded with astonishing brilliance—but he did it all with a joyous and infectious enthusiasm. With rare versatility, he was at one time or another to

Ebbets Field, September 30, 1955, the third game of the Dodger-Yankee World Series. Yankee pitcher Tom Morgan has just walked Pee Wee Reese with the bases loaded. Sandy Amoros is scoring and Duke Snider is coming to bat.

The Sandy Amoros catch in the seventh game of the 1955 World Series at Yankee Stadium. The umpire is John Flaherty.

Moments after pitching Brooklyn to its first World Championship, Podres is embraced by first baseman Gil Hodges, **left**, and outfielder Carl Furillo.

Dodger pitcher Johnny
Podres.

The scoreboard tells the story as Don Larsen delivers
the last pitch of his perfect game against Brooklyn in
the 1956 World Series. Behind Larsen is second
baseman Billy Martin.

Jackie Robinson after
announcing his retirement
from baseball in January of
1957.

lead the league in such disparate departments as batting average,
home runs (four times), triples (three times), and stolen bases
(four times).

It was in the field, however, that Mays's myriad talents were
most eye-catching. Not as graceful as DiMaggio (the only other
player in modern times in his class), Mays would run out from
under his hat, leap, slide, belly flop—and always get the ball. On one
occasion he made a catch that outdid even his usual miracles; it
was a running, **bare-handed** grab of a line drive in deep center.
When he returned to the dugout, the youngster was expecting
accolades. But Durocher had ordered the team to give him the
silent treatment. Finally, the frustrated Mays said to his poker-
faced manager, "Leo, didn't you see what I did out there?"

"No," Leo said. "So you'll just have to go out there and do it
again before I'll believe it."

Mays was one of two superstars to arrive in the big leagues in
1951. Not since Joe DiMaggio and Bob Feller in 1936 had a pair of
rookies appeared in the same year with such obvious greatness
stamped upon them. The other arrival was also a center fielder, also
with a New York team—the Yankees. His name was Mickey
Charles Mantle (the Mickey was for his father's favorite ballplayer
Mickey Cochrane—although in fact Cochrane's real first name was
actually Gordon, not Mickey).

Frank Lary, 20-game winner for Detroit in 1956 and 1961. Lary was always especially effective against the Yankees. He posted 7 wins and 1 loss against the New Yorkers in 1958, 28 and 13 lifetime.

Virgil Trucks, called Fire because of his blazing speed. He pitched two no-hitters for Detroit in 1952.

Pitcher Bob Lemon. Converted from an outfielder in 1946, Lemon went on to win 20 or more games seven times for the Cleveland Indians.

Early Wynn, one of a rare breed—a 300-game winner. He pitched in the American League for 23 years and five times was a 20-game winner. There was only one word for him on the mound: Tough.

Mantle was a switch-hitter with frightening power from either side of the plate. He also possessed a strong arm and had blinding speed afoot. Mantle's first season was DiMaggio's last, and so once more the Yankees managed to replace the irreplaceable.

Although it was DiMaggio he replaced, Mantle's qualities at bat were Ruthian. The Oklahoma-born youngster could hit a ball as far as any man who ever lived; his every appearance at bat had explosive potential. In 1953 he hit a home run in Washington that traveled an estimated 565 feet, the most phenomenal launching of a baseball since Ruth. Like Ruth and Foxx before him, Mantle faced many pitchers who simply were afraid to throw the ball over the plate to him, making him one of the most frequent "walkers" of all time.

Paul Richards: although never guiding a pennant winner, he was regarded as one of the finest baseball intellects in the game. He managed the Chicago White Sox and the Baltimore Orioles in the fifties, after having been a big league catcher in the thirties and forties.

Billy Pierce, ace left-hander for the White Sox. A 20-game winner in 1956 and 1957, he won 211 games overall.

Orestes "Minnie" Minoso, a popular and hard-hitting outfielder. Minoso batted over .300 eight times and three times led the American League in triples and in stolen bases.

Nelson Fox, star second baseman for the White Sox. He led the American League in hits four times. The league's most difficult strikeout year after year, Fox played in the big leagues 19 years and in that time struck out only 216 times in over 9,900 times at bat.

Harry Agganis, brilliant young Boston Red Sox first baseman who died in midseason in 1955 at the age of twenty-five. Recovering from pneumonia, he was suddenly stricken by a massive pulmonary embolism and died on June 27. Agganis had played in 25 games that year and was batting .313.

Above left:
Outfielder Charlie Maxwell, one of the favorites of Detroit fans in the late 1950s. One reason was because he usually hit home runs on Sundays when the crowds were largest.

Above right:
Harvey Kuenn, a solid, dependable, line-drive-hitting shortstop for the Tigers in the 1950s. Four times he led the American League in hits, three times in doubles, and once, in 1959, in batting with a .353 mark.

Left:
George Kell, one of the all-time top third basemen. Nine times a .300 hitter, Kell led the American League in batting in 1949 with a .343 average.

Joe Garagiola with the St. Louis
Cardinals in 1946. Later, he became
a popular television announcer.

Jimmy Piersall, one of the most
colorful ballplayers of all time.
Piersall had no peer when it came to
playing center field. His best year at
the plate was 1961, when he hit .322.

This sequence shows Jimmy Piersall trying to stretch a double into a triple. He slides into third where Yankee third baseman Clete Boyer already has the ball. Yelping at the sound of the "out" call, Jimmy begins a heated debate with umpire Joe Paparella.

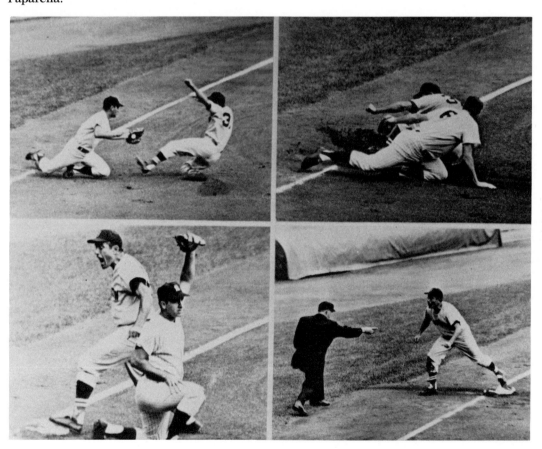

Despite a series of injuries that left him with badly damaged knees and deprived him of an even more glittering career, Mantle's statistics are impressive. He hit a lifetime total of 536 home runs; led the league in batting average, runs batted in, and home runs in 1956; and lost another batting title the following year when his .365 batting average was topped only by Ted Williams's astonishing .388.

The history of the New York Giants playing at home at the Polo Grounds is about to come to an end. The date is September 29, 1957. The pitcher is Bob Friend of the Pirates and the batter is Dusty Rhodes of the Giants. Rhodes hit the ball to short and was thrown out, ending the game. Whereupon the New York Giants slowly dissolved, to reappear the next year as the San Francisco Giants.

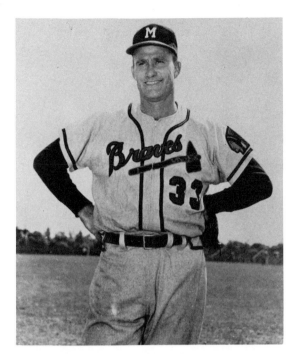

Lew Burdette, winner of three games for Milwaukee over the Yankees in the 1957 World Series.

Warren Spahn being gazed at with admiration from a very special source—his eight-year-old son Gregory. Spahn has just pitched and won the fourth game of the 1957 World Series against the Yankees.

Though the Yankees of the 1950s did not quite equal some of their predecessors, there was talent in abundance, nevertheless. Second to Mantle in offensive productivity was a squat, pleasantly homely and unlikely-looking athlete who possessed a natural swing, long-ball power, a winning personality, and a nickname to rank with Babe and Dizzy as a recognition factor: Lawrence Peter "Yogi" Berra.

While endearing himself for his humility and verbal fumbling (on Yogi Berra Night he thanked everyone "for making this night necessary"), Berra was most noted for his hitting and for his skills and shrewdness behind the plate. Awkward and uncertain when he first came to the big leagues, under the tutelage of Bill Dickey he eventually became one of the smoothest catchers in the game.

Other standouts on the Yankee teams that won the pennant in every year of the decade except '54 and '59 were Phil Rizzuto, Gerry Coleman, Hank Bauer, Gene Woodling, Gil McDougald, Bill

Eddie Mathews, greatest power-hitting third baseman in history. Four times he hit over 40 home runs, finishing with a lifetime total of 512.

Joe Adcock, hard-hitting first baseman on the Braves' pennant winners in 1957 and 1958. Adcock was the first man to hit a ball into the center field bleachers at the Polo Grounds in a major league game, on April 29, 1953. The drive carried an estimated 480 feet. Adcock's other big day in the major leagues occurred at Ebbets Field on July 31, 1954, when he hit four home runs and a double against the Dodgers.

The date: July 9, 1958. The place: Washington, D.C. The occasion: the United States Senate Anti-Trust and Monopoly Subcommittee is taking expert testimony with respect to baseball and the antitrust laws. The very self-assured witness is named Charles Dillon Stengel. Behind him on the left sits a colleague named Mantle while behind him on the right sits a gentleman named Williams (the only man in the august chamber not wearing a tie).

Skowron, Bobby Richardson, Tony Kubek, and Elston Howard. On the mound the Yankees had winners like Allie Reynolds, Vic Raschi, Eddie Lopat, Bob Turley, Don Larsen, and the greatest Yankee pitcher of all time—left-hander Whitey Ford, who was virtually unbeatable in a "money" game or any other game for that matter.

In 1953 there occurred something that was to prove a harbinger of the future. The uninterrupted continuity of National League membership was broken by the shifting of the Boston franchise to Milwaukee. The Braves attendance had been dwindling steadily until 1952, when the club drew fewer that 300,000. Gradually the Braves would revive in Milwaukee, soon becoming a contender, then a winner. The 1953 Braves had a muscular young slugger at third base, Eddie Mathews, who in his second year in the big leagues became the toast of Milwaukee when he hit 47 home runs and ended Ralph Kiner's seven-year reign as the league's home run champion.

A year later the St. Louis Browns dissolved, leaving behind an almost legendary history of mediocrity. The Browns then reappeared as the Baltimore Orioles. A decade later they became steady winners, proving that a change of name and address and a new suit of clothes can work wonders.

The Yankee onslaught of five straight pennants and World Championships finally came to an end in 1954. The Yankees died hard, winning 103 games, most ever for a non-pennant winner. Manager Al Lopez's Cleveland Indians, however, won an American League record 111 games. The Cleveland club had some fine hitters in Al Rosen, Larry Doby, and batting champ Bobby Avila. But it was pitching that carried the Indians in 1954, perhaps the greatest pitching staff ever. The Indians' pitching featured Bob Lemon, Early Wynn, Mike Garcia, Art Houtteman, an aging but still effective Bob Feller, and two relief specialists, lefty Don Mossi and righty Ray Narleski.

Following the adage that pitching will dominate a short series, the Indians went into the 1954 World Series against the Giants as

Roy McMillan of the Cincinnati Reds, one of the finest defensive shortstops of all time.

Ernie Banks, the premier power hitter among shortstops. Perhaps the most popular man ever to play for the Chicago Cubs, Banks had a lifetime total of 512 home runs. He was voted the National League's Most Valuable Player in 1958 and 1959.

Ted Kluszewski of the Cincinnati Reds, one of the strongest men in baseball, and one of the most likable. Seven times he hit over .300. His home run totals for 1953, '54, and '55 were 40, 49, and 47.

clear favorites. Baseball, however, has an adage for every occasion, and so another one had to be trundled out: "Anything can happen in a short series." In the 1954 World Series "anything" did happen. The Giants startled the baseball world with a four-game sweep. The victory was achieved by an unbelievable over-the-shoulder catch by Willie Mays on a booming clout by Vic Wertz in the opener, by game-winning pinch hits by reserve outfielder Dusty Rhodes, and by sturdy pitching by Giant aces Sal Maglie, Ruben Gomez, Johnny Antonelli, and a knuckleballing reliever named Hoyt Wilhelm.

Durocher's Giants had given the National League its first World Series victory since 1946, and Giant fans their first since 1933.

As if Cleveland did not already have enough pitching, they brought up the next year a tall young left-hander named Herb Score who came to the mound as naturally equipped as any pitcher who ever lived. Score possessed blinding speed and a wicked curve. He

Rocky Colavito was one of the American League's steadiest home run hitters for over a decade, mostly with Cleveland in the fifties and Detroit in the sixties. He reached his peak with 45 in 1961, when he drove across 140 runs. Colavito's greatest day came on June 10, 1959, when he hit four successive home runs for Cleveland in a game against the Baltimore Orioles. There was an angry uproar in Cleveland when he was traded to Detroit (for Harvey Kuenn) the day before the 1960 season opened.

was one of the few who fulfilled his promise instantly, winning 16 and then 20 games in his first two seasons, leading the league in strikeouts both years.

On May 7, 1957, however, in the first inning of a game against the Yankees, the twenty-three-year-old Score was struck in the eye by a line drive hit by Gil McDougald. Score was through for the year, and when he came back the next year something clearly was missing. Whether the damage caused by the injury was physical or mental, he never regained his greatness. The injury-aborted career of Herb Score is comparable to those of Smoky Joe Wood and Pete Reiser, making him one of the tantalizing "what-if" names of baseball lore.

The National League won the World Series again in 1955, setting off one of the most tumultuous victory celebrations in history. Overcoming the disappointments of 1950 and 1951, the great Brooklyn team won pennants in 1952 and 1953—only to be

Mickey Mantle.

turned back in October by the Yankees. Brooklyn was still without its first World Championship.

It all changed on October 4, 1955, in the seventh Series game at Yankee Stadium. The heroes were a young left-hander named Johnny Podres who had just gone through a mediocre season, and a speedy young Cuban named Sandy Amoros whose short career was destined to leave behind one exquisite moment.

That moment arrived in the decisive seventh game, in the bottom of the sixth inning, with the Dodgers leading, 2-0, behind Podres. The first two Yankees, Billy Martin and Gil McDougald, got on base. The batter was the dangerous Yogi Berra, a notorious pull hitter to right. Berra, however, crossed up everyone by lifting a high, slicing fly along the left-field line. Amoros, who had just been inserted in left field as a defensive replacement, went tearing after the ball. Racing head on toward the fence, he was several steps away from a collision when he stuck out his glove, made the catch, and fired a peg to Pee Wee Reese—who whirled and relayed it to Gil Hodges at first base, doubling off a surprised Gil McDougald.

That miraculous catch was the turning point. Thus reprieved, the gritty Podres kept fogging fastballs until it was over, and when he walked off the mound the borough of Brooklyn surged into an orgy of delirium that lasted through the night.

A year later, however, the Yankees turned it around and regained their championship in seven games against the Dodgers, and again "something" happened to Brooklyn in a World Series. This time it was to be more humiliating than an unassisted triple play or a dropped third strike; this time the calamity was total.

In the fifth game, at Yankee Stadium on October 8, 1956, Yankee pitcher Don Larsen finished what Floyd Bevens had started nine years earlier. Only this time it was no mere no-hitter. Larsen pitched a **perfect** game, turning back a power-packed Dodger lineup inning after inning, firing fastballs and curves and sliders from out of a then novel no-windup delivery. Purists still insist to this day that the last strike, to pinch hitter Dale Mitchell with two out in the ninth, was several inches outside. But umpire Babe Pinelli said it was not, and that was that.

Brooklyn would win no more pennants, but the Dodgers would. This became official after the 1957 season with the most startling franchise shifts in history. The tradition-rich Brooklyn Dodgers and New York Giants decided to abandon New York and set up shop in Los Angeles and San Francisco, respectively. Unlike the Boston Braves and St. Louis Browns, whose moves were compelled by lack of fan interest, both the Dodgers and Giants still maintained a strong following. They were, however, playing in outmoded ball parks located in deteriorating neighborhoods; also the virgin territory of the West Coast was too tempting to resist.

The Los Angeles Dodgers played their first few years in the Los Angeles Coliseum, a stadium designed for anything but baseball. Nevertheless, in their first year in California the Dodgers set a new team attendance record and were to go on year after year registering record-breaking attendance figures. The San Francisco Giants, playing at first in a minor league park that seated 23,000, also drew well. With the Braves already pulling large crowds in Milwaukee, and the Dodgers and Giants starting to do the same in California, the stage was now set for the further expansion that was to come in the next decade.

In Milwaukee the Braves rewarded their clamorous fans with pennants in 1957 and 1958. In '57 they won the World Series by defeating the Yankees in seven games, largely on the superlative pitching of a former Yankee farmhand, Lew Burdette, who won three complete game victories, two of them shutouts.

The Dodgers delighted many of the disgruntled fans they had left behind by finishing seventh in 1958, their first year in Los Angeles. The next season, however, Walter Alston's men resumed their winning ways, rising to the top once more and beating the Chicago White Sox in the 1959 World Series, after besting Milwaukee in a play-off. It was the third time in 14 seasons the Dodgers had finished in a tie for first place (and it would happen again in 1962, with the Giants).

On May 26, 1959, a slight, sad-faced left-hander for the Pittsburgh Pirates, Harvey Haddix, pitched what is undoubtedly one of baseball's most remarkable games. Pitching in Milwaukee against a team that included hitters like Eddie Mathews, Henry Aaron, Joe Adcock, Andy Pafko, Wes Covington, Del Crandall, and Johnny Logan, Haddix was methodical and perfect—for 12 full innings. Astonishingly, Haddix retired the first 36 men he faced. Unfortunately for Haddix, however, his Pittsburgh teammates could not score against Lew Burdette, which is why the game went on into extra innings.

The first crack in perfection was not Haddix's fault—his third baseman, Don Hoak, made an errant throw on a lead-off grounder in the bottom of the thirteenth. The perfect game was gone, but Haddix was still working on a no-hitter, the longest in baseball history. Eddie Mathews sacrificed the runner to second. Aaron was intentionally walked. The next batter was the powerful Joe Adcock. Adcock lined a ball toward right center that cleared the fence, but

Stan Musial.

because of some confusion on the base paths it was ruled a double and only one run allowed to score. But it did not matter. Haddix had lost—his perfect game, his no-hitter, his shutout, his game.

Almost as memorable as Haddix's performance was a question reportedly put to him after the game by a sportswriter: "Harvey, was this the greatest game you ever pitched?"

It was perhaps the greatest game anyone had ever pitched, and a sympathetic and appreciative fandom inundated Haddix with telegrams and letters of congratulations and consolation. But the most succinct and pointed message came from a college fraternity in the Midwest. It read, simply: "Dear Harvey: Tough shit."

"I was annoyed and upset when I first read it," Haddix said later, "but after thinking it over I decided that's exactly what it was."

A dazed and dejected Harvey Haddix in the dugout moments after losing his masterpiece.

Shibe Park, Philadelphia, 1974.

From Maz to the Miracle Mets
1960-1969

RECORDS, it has been said on occasion, are made to be broken. But at the start of 1960, who in his right mind would have predicted that before the sixties and seventies had passed into history the most cherished records of both Babe Ruth and Ty Cobb would be surpassed? The odds against such a parlay had to be a million to one. Include Bob Feller's most famous records and the odds would have multiplied a hundredfold.

And yet that is exactly what happened.

At the beginning of 1960, the following five records were considered virtually untouchable, at least for the foreseeable future.

Babe Ruth's 60 home runs in a season (1927). A few had come close: Hack Wilson with 56 home runs in 1930; Jimmie Foxx with 58 in 1932; and Hank Greenberg with 58 in 1938. But no one else had ever gotten as many as 55 home runs in one season.

Yet in 1961 Roger Maris hit 61.

Babe Ruth's 714 lifetime home runs (1914-1935). As the sixties got under way, there was no active player anywhere close to Ruth's magic number. Ted Williams was the closest, with 492, and he was on the verge of retirement. Young Henry Aaron had only 179.

Jim Bunning pitched for 17 years in the big leagues, mostly for the Tigers and Phillies, winning 224 games. On June 21, 1964, he pitched a perfect game against the New York Mets. It was always a wonder how he could field his position, since he typically ended his delivery completely off balance.

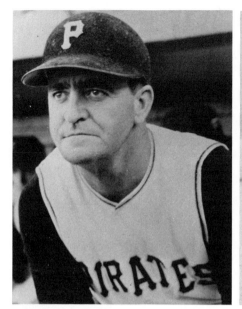

Danny Murtaugh, Pittsburgh manager during the 1960 World Series.

Tony Kubek has just been hit in the throat by a grounder off the bat of Bill Virdon in the eighth inning of the final game of the 1960 World Series. Second baseman Bobby Richardson has retrieved the ball and is calling for time out.

Elroy Face, star Pittsburgh relief pitcher from the early fifties to the late sixties. His phenomenal record of 18 wins and only 1 defeat in 1959 is still unmatched. Lifetime, he won 96 games in relief and saved another 193.

Yet on April 8, 1974, Henry Aaron hit home run number 715. He retired at the end of the 1976 season with a lifetime total of 755.

Ty Cobb's 96 stolen bases in a season (1915). Since Cobb, no one had stolen as many as 70 bases in a season, and since 1930 the highest had been Ben Chapman's 61 in 1931 and George Case's 61 in 1943. Base stealing appeared to be a lost art.

But in 1962 Maury Wills stole 104 bases. And in 1974 Lou Brock topped that with 118.

Ty Cobb's 892 lifetime stolen bases (1905-1928). At the start of the 1960 season, there was no active player with as many as even 200 lifetime stolen bases. It was a foregone conclusion that Cobb's record would stand forever. Lou Brock, a student at Southern University in Baton Rouge, Louisiana, had yet to play his first professional baseball game.

But on August 29, 1977, Lou Brock stole his 893rd base. By the end of the 1978 season he had stolen 917 bases.

Bill Mazeroski prances toward home plate after hitting his Series-winning home run in 1960. In the foreground Yankee manager Casey Stengel is an interested observer, while in the background pitcher Ralph Terry makes his lonely way toward the dressing room.

Bob Feller's 348 strikeouts in a season (1946). Feller had broken Rube Waddell's record of 343, which had lasted since 1904. Actually, after Feller fanned 348 in 1946 research into old box scores revealed that Waddell had actually struck out 349 in 1904. No matter—since Feller's performance, no pitcher had even reached the 300 mark.

In 1965, however, Sandy Koufax recorded 382 strikeouts. And in 1973 Nolan Ryan surpassed Koufax, with 383.

Several less well known but no less impressive marks were also erased in the sixties and seventies. The pitching record for the number of strikeouts in a nine-inning game, 18, had been held by Bob Feller since 1938. Sandy Koufax tied it in 1959, and again in 1962. But it was broken, with a new record of 19 strikeouts, not once, not twice, but **three** times: by Steve Carlton in 1969, by Tom Seaver in 1970, and by Nolan Ryan in 1974.

To cap off all the rest: as the sixties began, only two men in history had pitched as many as three no-hitters—Cy Young and Bob Feller. But in the sixties Sandy Koufax pitched **four** no-hitters, and then Nolan Ryan did the same in the seventies.

As though to give a preview of what was in store, the decade opened on a high note with the Yankees and Pittsburgh Pirates playing one of baseball's most dramatic World Series. After losing the American League pennant to the Chicago White Sox in 1959, the Yankees started another winning streak in 1960 that was to reach five straight league titles before the dynasty would finally crumble in 1965. These were the years of Elston Howard behind the plate, Moose Skowron and then Joe Pepitone at first base, Bobby Richardson at second, Tony Kubek at shortstop, Clete Boyer at third, and mainly Mantle and Maris in the outfield. Whitey Ford and Ralph Terry were the top pitchers, helped by Al Downing, Jim Bouton, and others.

The Pirates, in their first World Series since 1927, also had a well-balanced team: Dick Stuart at first base, Bill Mazeroski at second, Dick Groat at short, Don Hoak at third, and Bob Skinner, Bill Virdon, and Roberto Clemente in the outfield. Vernon Law, Bob Friend, Harvey Haddix, and Elroy Face were the pitching mainstays, Smoky Burgess the catcher.

The 1960 World Series went the full seven games, and it was the seventh that will never be forgotten. Pittsburgh took a 4-0 lead in the first two innings and seemed like sure winners. But the Yankees rebounded and **they** then seemed like sure winners, with the score 7-4 in New York's favor as the Pirates came to bat in the bottom of the eighth inning. With a man on first, Bill Virdon hit what appeared to be a double-play ball at shortstop Tony Kubek.

Roger Maris as a Yankee.   And then as a Cardinal.

→
Willie McCovey, one of the few players in the
history of baseball to hit over 500 home runs.
He came within inches of being the hero of
the 1962 World Series.

Opposite page, top:

Whitey Ford, greatest of all Yankee pitchers.
He won 236 and lost 106 over his career for a
winning percentage of .690. His peak year
was 1961, when he won 25 and lost 4.

Opposite page, bottom:

It is October 1, 1961, the final day of the
season, and a physically and mentally
exhausted Roger Maris has just hit record-
breaking home run number 61.

Juan Marichal, six times a 20-game winner for the San Francisco Giants in the sixties. He won 243 games over his 16-year career.

Maury Wills.

Second baseman Bump Wills, Maury's son, broke into the major leagues in 1977, only five years after his father had retired.

But the ball took a bad hop and hit Kubek in the throat, sending him sprawling. That opened the floodgates, and before the inning was over Pittsburgh scored five runs, climaxed by reserve catcher Hal Smith's three-run homer. The score was now 9-7 in Pittsburgh's favor, going into the ninth inning, and again the Pirates appeared to have it sewed up. But the Yankees came back once more and scored two runs in the top of the ninth to tie the game at 9-9.

The apex was reached in the bottom of the ninth: Ralph Terry pitching for New York, second baseman Bill Mazeroski the first man up for Pittsburgh. Maz swung at Terry's second pitch and drove the ball over the left-field wall, winning the game 10-9 and the World Championship for the Pittsburgh Pirates.

Felipe

Matty

The hard-hitting Alou brothers. Throughout their careers, they got more base hits than the three DiMaggio brothers (although not as many as Paul and Lloyd Waner). In 1963 all three played for the San Francisco Giants.

Pitcher Jim Bouton won 21 game the Yankees in 1963 and 18 in 19 then lost his fastball, was sent do the minors, wrote a best-selling b (**Ball Four**), and finally retired fr game in 1970 at the age of thirty-But years later, determined to co back, he gave up a lucrative TV sportscaster's job and doggedly knocked around for several years low minor leagues trying to perfe knuckleball: here, in 1975, the on time Yankee star waits out a rain with the Portland Mavericks in th Northwest League. His tenacity w rewarded, however, when he asto ished everyone by making it back big leagues with the Atlanta Brav late in 1978, at the age of thirty-n And when he defeated the Giants September 14, 1978, it was his fir major league win since July 11, 1

Jesus

After, the Series, Charles Dillon Stengel—born in 1890 and winner of 10 Yankee pennants (and 7 World Championships) in 12 years—was deposed as Yankee manager because of his age and replaced by Ralph Houk. "I guess this means they fired me," Casey said. "I'll never make the mistake of being seventy again."

In 1961 the American League expanded from 8 to 10 teams and replaced the traditional 154-game schedule with a new 162-game format. (The National League followed suit the next year.) The new schedule produced unexpected fireworks because 1961 happened to be the year Mickey Mantle and Roger Maris picked to challenge Babe Ruth's sacrosanct record of 60 home runs in a single season. But what is a season? Controversy mounted as Mantle and Maris came within hailing distance of Ruth: since the season was now eight games longer, if one of them topped 60

Bill White and Orlando Cepeda handled first base with aplomb for the St. Louis Cardinals from 1959 through 1968. Each had a distinguished career with other teams as well, White with the Phillies and Cepeda with the Giants.

Orlando Cepeda.

Bill White.

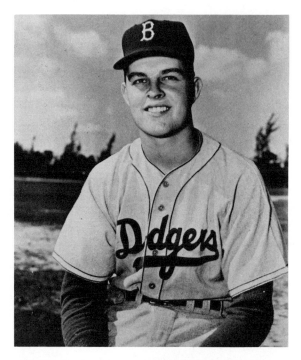

Don Drysdale with the Dodgers in 1957. In 1960 his fastball was timed at 95.3 miles an hour (and he did not hesitate to let opposing batters know it). In 1968 he pitched 58 consecutive shutout innings, breaking a record that had been set by Walter Johnson in 1913. During his 14-year career with the Dodgers he won 209 games.

Hard-hitting outfielder Tommy Davis led the National League in batting in 1962 and 1963.

Sandy Koufax.

would it really be a new record? Amid excited debate, Commissioner Ford Frick ruled that if Ruth's figure were surpassed within 154 games, then there was no question, of course, about its being a new record; if it were surpassed in a later game, then it would still be a new record but modified by an asterisk, denoting that the accomplishment required more than the traditional 154 games.

Mantle's bid faded in September, due to injuries, and he ended the season with 54 home runs. But Maris persevered, in the face of rising odds and unbearable pressure. He hit number 59 in the 154th game, thus falling one shy of Ruth's figure in the same number of games.

But then, in one last almost superhuman explosion, he blasted two more over the fence in the extended portion of the season, with the prized number 61 coming in Yankee Stadium, off Tracy Stallard of the Red Sox, in his second time at bat on October 1, the final day of the season.

Roger Eugene Maris was twenty-seven years old at the time. Uncommunicative with strangers, accustomed to living life on his own terms, he valued, above all, privacy and independence. As he

Walter Alston managed the Dodgers to seven pennants and four World Series victories between the mid-fifties and the midseventies. As a player, however, his career was brief: he came to bat once with the St. Louis Cardinals in 1936, struck out, and that was that.

Ken Boyer, the St. Louis Cardinals' third baseman for 11 years, from 1955 through 1965. In eight of those years he batted in 90 or more runs.

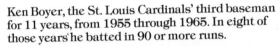

Lou Brock. Not only the most prolific base stealer in the history of baseball, but also one of the best clutch hitters. In the 1964 World Series he batted .300, in the 1967 Series .414, and in the 1968 Series .464.

Bob Gibson.

Line-drive-hitting Tony Oliva,
batting champion of the American
League in 1964, 1965, and 1971.

Catcher John Roseboro,
left, and pitcher Camilo
Pascual. Roseboro, long-
time Dodger catcher
(1957-67) came to the
Twins near the end of his
career. Pascual pitched 18
years in the big leagues,
mostly with Washington
and Minnesota.

Pitcher Jim Kaat won over 260 games in the major leagues, mostly with the Minnesota Twins. He won 18 games to help the Twins win the pennant in 1965, and then 25 the following year.

approached number 60, he found himself losing both. He became upset over the merciless invasion of his privacy by the media, bewildered by the public resentment that built up as he, an unknown, dared challenge the most hallowed of all records. On a typical day half the crowd would be applauding Maris, the other half taunting him, rooting for Babe Ruth. Embittered, he finally retreated behind a protective wall of sullen truculence. When at last he seized the Holy Grail, on Octber 1, 1961, it turned to ashes in his hands.

Maris played with the Yankees for five more years, more often booed than cheered. He responded, jaw set, by deliberately going

Harmon Killebrew hit 573 home runs during his 22 years in the American League, stretching from 1954 through 1975. He hit one every 14.2 times at bat, a frequency exceeded only by Babe Ruth (who homered once every 11.8 times at bat) and by Ralph Kiner (once every 14.1 times).

for singles and doubles, avoiding the home runs that had been both his glory and his cross. Then he was traded to the St. Louis Cardinals, where he played for two years, happy to be over-shadowed by Bob Gibson, Lou Brock, and Orlando Cepeda. After the 1968 season he retired from baseball, thirty-four years of age, and returned to the hearthside that he had never wanted to leave in the first place.

The Yankees continued as American League pennant winners in 1961, '62, '63, and '64, beating Cincinnati in the 1961 World Series and then squeaking past the San Francisco Giants in 1962. The 1962 Series went the full seven games and was decided by a 1-0 seventh game Yankee victory in which Ralph Terry outpitched Jack Sanford. In the bottom of the ninth inning of the seventh game, with the Yankees ahead 1-0, the Giants got men on second and third with two out. Next batter: 6-foot-4-inch Willie McCovey. Ralph Terry, on the mound, could not help but shudder as he remembered throwing that home-run ball to Mazeroski two years earlier. And it almost happened again. With the count one ball and one strike, McCovey smashed a vicious rising line drive toward right center field—second baseman Bobby Richardson speared it instinctively, and the World Series was over. Had McCovey's shot been a few inches higher, or Richardson's reflexes less than

Frank Robinson, Most Valuable Player in the National League in 1961 and in the American League in 1966. In October of 1974 he became the first black to be hired as a major league manager (and in June of 1977 the first to be fired).

perfect, the Series would also have been over—but the Giants would have won it.

The big story of 1962, however, was not the World Series, and not even the fact that Casey Stengel's brand-new Mets brought National League baseball back to New York; it was Dodger shortstop Maury Wills's 104 stolen bases, breaking Ty Cobb's 47-year-old record for the most stolen bases in a season (96). It had taken Cobb 156 games to set the record in 1915—Detroit played two tie games that year—and it was in game number 156 that Wills both tied and passed Cobb's mark. Then he stole seven more to wind up with 104—a record that everyone assumed would surely stand at least another 47 years. (Actually, of course, it lasted only 12.)

Maurice Morning Wills, a wiry switch-hitting shortstop, was born in Washington, D.C., one of 13 children. Although 5 feet 10 inches tall and 170 pounds, he looked frail, and his size—as well as his color—kept him in the minors almost nine years before the Dodgers finally gave him a chance in 1959, when he was twenty-six years old. Even so, he played 14 years in the major leagues and became perhaps the most skillful base stealer of all time: he was

Three Chicago Cubs Stars of the Sixties

Pitcher Ferguson Jenkins won over 230 major league games. Seven times he won 20 or more.

Outfielder Billy Williams played in 1,117 consecutive games, the all-time National League record, and hit over 400 home runs.

Third baseman Ron Santo, a diabetic all the while he was in the big leagues, drove in 90 or more runs eight times.

thrown out trying to steal only 13 times the year he stole 104 bases, whereas Cobb was thrown out 38 times when he stole his 96 (and Lou Brock was caught 33 times in 1974, when he stole 118).

As though to prove Satchel Paige's axiom—"Don't look back, something might be gaining on you"—the year Wills broke Cobb's record, 1962, was twenty-three-year-old Lou Brock's first full season in the majors. Little did Wills realize that the Chicago Cubs' rookie outfielder, with only 16 stolen bases that season, would outdo him with 118 steals a dozen years later.

Luis Aparicio, Venezuelan-born shortstop for the Chicago White Sox from 1956 through 1962, for the Baltimore Orioles from 1963 through 1967, for the White Sox again from 1968 through 1970, and for the Red Sox from 1971 through 1973. During his 18-year major league career Luis stole over 500 bases, leading the American League in stolen bases nine times.

Jim Lonborg shutting out the Cardinals with only one hit in the second game of the 1967 World Series. (The shortstop in the background is Rico Petrocelli.)

Carl Michael Yastrzemski, the Pride of New England, in 1967.

The mighty Yankee dynasty started to totter in 1963 and 1964. They won the pennant both years but lost the World Series to the Los Angeles Dodgers in 1963 and to the St. Louis Cardinals in 1964. After that they fell apart completely, finishing sixth in 1965 and a dismal last in 1966 (for the first time since 1912).

Their place at the pinnacle was taken by two National League teams, the Los Angeles Dodgers and the St. Louis Cardinals, with one or the other winning the National League pennant every year from 1963 through 1968 and the World Series in four of those six years. Both had outstanding teams during the sixties: the Dodgers with John Roseboro behind the plate and an all switch-hitting infield consisting of Wes Parker at first, Jim Lefebvre at second,

Sam McDowell led the American League in strike-outs five times, fanning 325 in 1965.

Hoyt Wilhelm threw his knuckleball—really held by the fingertips—for 21 major league seasons, from 1952 through 1972. He was still pitching in the big leagues at the age of forty-nine. He participated in a record 1,070 games, almost all in relief, winning 143 and saving 227 more.

Maury Wills at shortstop, and Jim Gilliam at third. In the outfield were Tommy Davis, Willie Davis, Ron Fairly, Frank Howard, and Lou Johnson. And, above all, the Dodger pitching: Sandy Koufax, Don Drysdale, Ron Perranoski, Johnny Podres, Claude Osteen, and Don Sutton.

The Cardinals were equally impressive: Tim McCarver catching, Bill White and then Orlando Cepeda at first base, Ken Boyer and then Mike Shannon at third, and Julian Javier, Dick Groat, and Dal Maxvill in the middle of the infield; in the outfield Lou Brock, Curt Flood, Mike Shannon, and later Roger Maris. The pitching was handled by Bob Gibson, Curt Simmons, Nelson Briles, and young Steve Carlton, not yet the brilliant 20-game winner he would later become.

Four Mainstays of the Detroit Tigers in the Sixties

First baseman Norm Cash had his best year in 1961, when he hit 41 home runs, drove in 132 runs, and led the American League with a .361 batting average.

Husky outfielder Willie Horton was a fixture in the Detroit lineup for over a decade.

Al Kaline amassed over 3,000 hits during his 22 years in right field. He led the league with a .340 batting average in 1955, before reaching his twenty-first birthday.

Denny McLain won 31 games in 1968, the first 30-game winner since Dizzy Dean in 1934. He won another 24 in 1969, but thereafter his career went into a tailspin.

Mickey Lolich, hero of the
1968 World Series.

Hawk Harrelson in 1966,
with a few of his many golf
trophies. The Hawk hit 35
home runs for the Red Sox
in 1968 and led the
American League in runs
batted in that year.
However, a few years later
he retired from baseball, at
the age of twenty-nine, to
become a professional
golfer.

Jim and Gaylord Perry, the winningest pitching brothers of all time. Jim won 215 games from 1959 through 1975, and Gaylord won 267 from the early sixties through 1978—including 21 in 1978, when he was forty years old! In 1978 Gaylord also became only the third pitcher in baseball history to reach 3,000 lifetime strikeouts (the first two were Walter Johnson and Bob Gibson). Jim won the Cy Young Award as the best pitcher in the American League in 1970 and Gaylord won it twice: in the American League in 1972 and then in the National League in 1978.

Jim

Gaylord

Sandy Koufax and Bob Gibson, a left-hander and a right-hander, a Jew and a black, were in their prime at that time, and at their best no one in the history of baseball—not even Christy Mathewson or Walter Johnson or Grover Cleveland Alexander or Lefty Grove or Bob Feller—was any better.

Sanford Koufax—6 feet 2 inches tall and 200 pounds but deceptively slim in appearance, shy, reflective, son of middle-class Jewish parents—grew up in Brooklyn and joined the Dodgers in 1955 at the age of nineteen. He received a $14,000 bonus, but for a long time it seemed like money down the drain. Sandy had awe-inspiring speed but little control and even less patience with his own failings. In 1960, after six years, his record was only 36 wins and 40 losses, and it looked very much as though the Dodgers should have saved their money and Koufax should have followed his original inclination and become an architect.

But then, in 1961, it all started to come together and soon thereafter he became the Sandy Koufax those who saw will never forget: four no-hit games, the last one a perfect game; 382

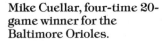

Mike Cuellar, four-time 20-game winner for the Baltimore Orioles.

strikeouts in 1965; three-time winner of 25 or more games; five consecutive years league leader in earned run average; three times unanimously voted the Cy Young Award as the best pitcher in baseball.

And as quickly as it began, it ended. On November 18, 1966, after his best season ever, Sandy Koufax announced that he would never pitch again.

A traumatic arthritic condition in his left elbow had become progressively worse. Before pitching he had to be given injections, during a game his arm would swell as much as an inch, and afterward his elbow had to be packed in ice. Doctors said that to continue pitching would result in serious permanent injury. So at the peak of his career, Sandy Koufax, not yet thirty-one years old, smiled wanly and said farewell. It is tragic that he was forced to retire so early. Always modest, he never thought he was as good as people said. In retrospect, though, he looks even better

Bob Gibson was an inch shorter than Koufax and weighed 10 pounds less, but in a baseball uniform he looked bigger. He was born on the wrong side of the tracks in Omaha, Nebraska, in 1935, the seventh child of an extremely poor family. Aloof, proud, deeply aware of poverty, racial prejudice, and other social inequities, Gibson pitched with an intensity that seemed to express a grim determination to prove everyone wrong who had ever put people down because of the color of their skin.

And prove them wrong he did: 251 victories over a brilliant 17-year career with the St. Louis Cardinals, more victories than any other Cardinal pitcher in history; 3,117 strikeouts, the first pitcher since Walter Johnson to record over 3,000 lifetime strikeouts; an earned run average of 1.12 in 1968, the lowest ever for a National League pitcher with over 300 innings pitched in a season; a record seven consecutive World Series victories, including one in 1968 in which he struck out 17—tops for any World Series pitcher; twice Cy Young Award winner as the best pitcher in the league; and the National League's Most Valuable Player in 1968.

In the 1963 World Series, the Los Angeles Dodgers—led by Sandy Koufax, Don Drysdale, Maury Wills, and Tommy Davis—humiliated the Yankees by winning four straight games. The once-mighty Yankees could score only four runs in the entire Series. A year later it was the Cardinals—with Bob Gibson, Tim McCarver, Ken Boyer, and Lou Brock—who took New York's measure, although this time it required the full seven games. Actually, the Cards were lucky to be in the Series at all in 1964, for this was the year that Philadelphia Phillies fans remember all too well; the

The end of the trail. Jim Ray Hart starred at third base for the Giants from 1963 to 1972, and then played with the Yankees for most of 1973 and part of 1974. This picture was snapped on May 29, 1974, moments after he has been informed that the Yankees will no longer need his services—that he is being released. (The equally crestfallen bystander is reporter Murray Chass of the **New York Times**.)

Cleon Jones.

Jerry Koosman.

Phillies had a six-and-a-half game lead in the National League with only two weeks left in the season, and then proceeded to blow it by losing 10 games in a row!

It was the Dodgers' turn again in 1965, as they alternated with the Cardinals as National League pennant winners, but this time they met not the Yankees in the World Series—New York ended sixth—but the Minnesota Twins, with their first pennant ever. The big guns for Minnesota were right fielder Tony Oliva and third baseman Harmon Killebrew, and an imposing pair they were. Oliva, born in Cuba, sleek as a greyhound, winner of three batting crowns over his career; and Killebrew, Idaho-born, imposing as a Brahman bull, six-time American League home run leader, with a total of 573 home runs during his 22 illustrious years in the American League. But Koufax was too much for the Twins—after sitting out the opening Series game because of Yom Kippur, a Jewish holiday, Sandy shut out Minnesota in the fifth and seventh games, striking out 10 each time.

The demise of the Yankees opened the way for new cream to rise to the top in the American League. The pennant-winning

Three reasons why the New York Mets won pennants in 1969 and 1973. Cleon Jones hit .340 in 1969; Jerry Koosman won 17 games in 1969 and 14 in 1973; and Tug McGraw won or saved 20 games in relief in 1969 and 30 in 1973.

Tug McGraw.

Tom Seaver.

Twins were succeeded by the Baltimore Orioles in 1966, and in turn by the Boston Red Sox and then the Detroit Tigers. As a result, outstanding players who had toiled for years in relative obscurity began to receive the acclaim they merited as they participated in World Series action: stars like Frank Robinson, Brooks Robinson, Dave McNally, Jim Palmer, Boog Powell, Carl Yastrzemski, Rico Petrocelli, Al Kaline, Norm Cash, and Mickey Lolich, to mention but a few. (Others, like Ernie Banks, Jim Bunning, Ferguson Jenkins, Juan Marichal, Gaylord Perry, and Billy Williams played all or virtually all of their careers with also-rans and never did receive the national attention they deserved.)

Frank and Brooks Robinson, for example, had been outstanding players for a decade before Baltimore made it to the World Series in 1966, but to the general public they were hardly household names. Frank had come up with the Cincinnati Reds in 1956 and was Rookie of the Year that year, and the National League's Most Valuable Player in 1961, but Mantle and Maris had overshadowed everyone that year. Inexplicably traded by the Reds to Baltimore after the 1965 season, Robinson promptly retaliated by leading the American League in batting average, home runs, and runs batted in (the coveted triple crown). Named the American League's Most Valuable Player in 1966, he thereby became the only player ever to win that honor in both leagues. Eventually, in 1975, he became major league baseball's first black manager.

Brooks Robinson was similarly neglected for years before finally gaining recognition as the finest third baseman of his generation, possibly of all time. When he eventually retired in 1977, after more than 20 acrobatic years with the Orioles, he held just about every fielding record for third basemen worth having. Even old-timers, for decades convinced that no one could possibly match—much less surpass—Pie Traynor and Billy Cox as third basemen, began to waver, no longer so sure that Pie and Billy were alone at the top.

The Baltimore Orioles won the 1966 American League pennant in a romp and then buried the Los Angeles Dodgers, Koufax and all, in four straight World Series games. No matter how good the Dodger pitching, it didn't matter, because after scoring two runs early in the first game the Dodgers didn't score another one in the entire Series. Shut out in three straight games, they made the fewest hits (17) and scored the fewest runs (2) of any team in World Series history. Shortly after the Series ended, Koufax retired and both Maury Wills and Tommy Davis were traded; it would be eight years before Los Angeles could win another pennant.

Seaver and catcher Jerry Grote.

While the Orioles were winning in 1966, the Boston Red Sox were finishing a dreary ninth. In 1967, however, to everyone's astonishment, the Red Sox edged out the White Sox, Twins, and Tigers to win the American League championship on the final day of the season. The Impossible Dream, it was called, from ninth place to the pennant in one year, and it was transformed from a dream into reality by the steady pitching of Jim Lonborg and, above all, by the daily batting and fielding pyrotechnics of an erstwhile Notre Dame student, son of a Long Island potato farmer, Carl Michael Yastrzemski.

It is obviously impossible for one man to win a pennant. And yet if it has ever been done it was done in 1967, and the man who did it was Boston left-fielder Carl Yastrzemski. Intelligent, moody, charismatic, he virtually carried the entire team on his back through the 1967 season—indeed, carried it up to within one game of a World Championship.

Yaz led the league in hits, batting average, runs scored, runs batted in, and inspiration. He tied Harmon Killebrew for the league lead in home runs. He made hard-to-believe catches in left field and threw base runners out when it counted. In the closing two weeks of the season, with four teams nose to nose, he slammed 23

Receiving the Cy Young Award in 1973 from Joseph Durso of the **New York Times**.

hits in 44 times at bat, including 4 doubles and 5 home runs, and drove in 16 runs. In the final two games of the season, with the title on the line, he got 7 hits in 8 times at bat, including a game-winning home run.

The 1967 World Series went seven games, but after all was said and done the Cardinals' Roger Maris, Lou Brock, and Bob Gibson rudely combined to interrupt Boston's Impossible Dream just short of an idyllic ending. Yaz hit .400, with 10 hits, including 2 doubles and 3 home runs, and threw out 2 base runners. But Roger Maris, in his first season in St. Louis, happy to be away from New York, drove in 7 runs, and Lou Brock hit .414 and stole a record 7 bases. And above all Bob Gibson—scowling on the mound as though defying the world—won the first, fourth, and seventh games, allowing only 14 hits and striking out 26.

How could Lou Brock and Bob Gibson possibly be stopped? That was the problem facing the Detroit Tigers as they prepared to meet the St. Louis Cardinals in the 1968 World Series. Detroit had its own pitching ace, Denny McLain, the first 30-game winner since Dizzy Dean in 1934. McLain won 31 and lost only 6, and he had a hard-hitting team behind him: Al Kaline, Norm Cash, Dick McAuliffe, Jim Northrup, Willie Horton, Mickey Stanley, Gates

Mets' right fielder Ron Swoboda's famous catch in the ninth inning of the fourth game of the 1969 World Series.

Swoboda dives for a sinking line drive off the bat of Brooks Robinson...grabs the ball just before it hits the ground...rolls over...

...and triumphantly holds up his gloved hand clutching the baseball.

Brown, and Bill Freehan, among others. In addition, pitching in McLain's shadow was a carefree paunchy left-hander, Mickey Lolich, with a fastball every bit as swift as Denny's.

But Brock and Gibson picked up right where they had left off the previous year. Brock hit .464, with two home runs, and stole seven more bases. Gibson, for his part, shut out the Tigers in the opening game, striking out a record 17, and then came back to strike out 10 more in winning the fourth game. The Tigers appeared to be clearly outclassed. However, although McLain faltered, little-noticed Mickey Lolich kept the pace, winning the second and fifth games for Detroit.

As the seventh and deciding game began, with a match-up of Gibson vs. Lolich, the intense Cardinal right-hander had a string of seven consecutive World Series victories behind him and looked unbeatable. In the seventh inning, however, with the game scoreless, Cardinal center fielder Curt Flood, one of the best defensive outfielders in the business, misjudged a line drive off the bat of Jim Northrup and let in two runs. For all practical purposes that was the ball game, and the World Series too. And so it turned out to be not Robert Gibson or Dennis Dale McLain who won three games in the 1968 World Series—but twenty-eight-year-old, happy-go-lucky Michael Stephen Lolich!

Two major changes came into effect with the 1969 season. First, both leagues expanded from ten to twelve teams (Montreal and San Diego joining the National League, Seattle and Kansas City the American League), with each league splitting into an Eastern and a Western Division. Henceforth, each league's division winners would meet in a three out of five Championship Series, better known as play-offs, the winners to meet in the World Series.

Second, measures were taken to assist the batter in his eternal duel with the pitcher. Pitching had come to dominate both leagues and too few runs were being scored, in the opinion of those whose primary interest lies in attendance figures and gate receipts. In 1968 only five National Leaguers were able to hit over .300, and only one American Leaguer—Carl Yastrzemski had led the American League in batting with a .301 average, the lowest league-leading average of all time. To rectify the imbalance, the pitching mound was lowered five inches and the strike zone shrunk. Instead of from the top of the shoulder to the bottom of the knee, the strike zone was contracted to from the armpit to the top of the knee. Both changes handicapped the pitcher and helped the batter.

But all this became trivial compared to what happened on the field in 1969. For that was the year the New York Mets, of all teams, won not only the National League Eastern Division title but the play-offs after that—and then the World Series as well!

Born in 1962, when the National League expanded to 10 teams, midwifed by Charles Dillon Stengel, the Mets had never previously finished higher than ninth—which is where they ended the 1968 season, 24 games out of first place. Few expected much more in 1969. But manager Gil Hodges knew he had the nucleus of a better team than people realized in young pitchers Tom Seaver, Jerry Koosman, Gary Gentry, Ron Taylor, Nolan Ryan, and Tug McGraw, catcher Jerry Grote, shortstop Bud Harrelson, and outfielders Cleon Jones and Tommie Agee. With them as the foundation, Hodges skillfully platooned infielders Ed Kranepool, Donn Clendenon, Ken Boswell, Al Weis, Ed Charles, and Wayne Garrett, and outfielders Ron Swoboda and Art Shamsky. By early September Hodges had guided the Mets to first place, and from there they went on to sweep three straight from the Atlanta Braves in the National League play-offs.

The early years of the Mets—from 1962 through 1968—were marked as much by laughter as by tears. Marvelous Marv Throneberry at first base provided more than his share of both. In one game Marvelous Marv hit two triples and both times was called out by the umpires for failing to touch second base. The second time it happened Manager Stengel rushed out of the dugout to protest, but before he got very far first base coach Cookie Lavagetto stopped him: "Don't bother, Casey," he said, "he didn't touch first base either."

But in 1969 things were different and they became known as the Miracle Mets. Their guiding light was George Thomas Seaver, twenty-four years old, from Fresno, California. Brought up in a financially comfortable, athletically inclined family, where integrity was emphasized as much as sports, Tom Seaver joined the Mets in 1967. Bright, articulate, with a fastball that hummed, for the decade he was with the Mets he was The Franchise: Rookie of the Year in 1967 and three times Cy Young Award winner as the league's best pitcher. In 1969 he won 25 games and lost 7, but his infectious enthusiasm was as important as his fastball in bringing the Mets to the World Series.

On paper, the Baltimore Orioles had a better team than the New York Mets, with stars like Brooks and Frank Robinson, Boog Powell, Paul Blair, Mark Belanger, and outstanding pitchers like Mike Cuellar, Dave McNally, and Jim Palmer. Cuellar was in the first of his four 20-victory seasons, McNally in the second of his four, and Jim Palmer was already showing the form that would earn him three Cy Young Awards and the distinction of being the American League's best pitcher in the seventies.

But faith and passion have been known to overcome even bigger obstacles than Boog Powell, the Orioles' massive first baseman, and that they did so once again, in October of 1969, came as no surprise to those who believe in fate and destiny. The Mets took the Series with seeming ease, four games to one, by virtue of excellent pitching, clutch hitting, and brilliant catches at crucial moments by outfielders Tommie Agee and Ron Swoboda.

And thus the sixties closed as dramatically as they had opened: from Bill Mazeroski's electrifying drive over the left-field wall on October 13, 1960, to Cleon Jones's game-ending catch of an easy fly ball off the bat of Oriole second baseman Dave Johnson at 3:17 P.M. on October 16, 1969, at that instant making the New York Mets the Champions of the World.

Roberto Clemente.

Dollar Decade
The $eventie$

MANAGER EARL WEAVER and his Baltimore Orioles were less
than ecstatic about having acted as foils for the Mets in the 1969
World Series. they proceeded to take their frustrations out on the
rest of the American League in 1970, winning the Eastern
Division title by a wide margin and then trouncing Minnesota
three straight in the play-offs.

Somewhat tougher opposition faced them in the World Series,
in the form of Pete Rose, Johnny Bench, Tony Perez, and the rest of
freshman manager Sparky Anderson's Cincinnati Reds. But the
Big Red Machine was not yet as imposing as it would become in
later years, and the Orioles got sweet revenge on the National
League without too much trouble, four games to one.

Although Baltimore's Boog Powell, Frank Robinson, and
Brooks Robinson each hit two home runs, the star of the 1970
Series was Brooks. He batted .429 and drove in six runs, but above
all he opened the eyes of a nationwide television audience by his
sensational play around third base. Time and again, he turned sure
hits into outs with diving, leaping, tumbling catches, followed by
clothesline throws to first base from prone, kneeling, or off-balance
positions. His defensive genius had made him a hero in Baltimore
for a decade, but now, for the first time, he was properly appreciated
by the nation at large. From that time on, Brooks Robinson was

Brooks Robinson in the late fifties.

A diving catch of Johnny Bench's liner ends the sixth inning of the third game of the 1970 World Series.

Brooks Robinson in the
mid - seventies.

Roberto Clemente triples off the left-center field wall in the first inning of the sixth game of the 1971 World Series. (Jim Palmer is the Baltimore pitcher, Ellie Hendricks the catcher, and John Kibler the umpire.)

linked with Pie Traynor and Billy Cox as the standard against which future generations of third basemen would be judged.

Just as the 1970 World Series made a national figure of Brooks Robinson, the following Series did the same for the Pittsburgh Pirates' long-time right fielder, Roberto Clemente. Sensitive, mercurial, his feelings easily hurt, his emotions always close to the surface, Roberto Clemente was born in Carolina, Puerto Rico, in 1934, the seventh child of a poor rural family. He joined the Pirates in 1955, not yet turned twenty-one, and four times thereafter he led the league in batting, three times he hit over .350, and his arm in right field was known around the circuit as the strongest and most accurate in baseball.

Clemente resented the fact that he had never received the recognition that was his due, and he felt, not unreasonably, that it had something to do with his being both black and Puerto Rican, a heritage of which he was extremely proud. A veteran of seventeen years in the big leagues, thirty-seven years of age, Roberto eagerly looked forward to the 1971 World Series as a last chance to show the world that he was as good as the best—and just possibly even a bit better.

Curt Flood in front of the Federal
Courthouse in New York on June 1, 1970,
as his case against organized baseball's
reserve clause is about to be argued.

Vida Blue and pitching coach Bill Posedel in 1971, when Blue won the Cy Young Award as the American League's best pitcher and was voted the league's Most Valuable Player as well.

The Pirates entered the Series decided underdogs. Facing them were the Baltimore Orioles, winners of three consecutive American League pennants, the same team that had overwhelmed Cincinnati the previous year and was just as powerful in 1971— powerful enough to take Oakland's measure with three straight victories in the American League play-offs. But with two sparkling pitching performances from Steve Blass, and the thirty-seven-year-old Clemente playing his heart out, Pittsburgh won the 1971 World Series from Baltimore in seven games. Clemente batted .414, with seven singles, two doubles, a triple, and two home runs. He left no doubt whatsoever about his greatness.

The following year, on September 30, 1972, Clemente doubled off Mets left-hander Jon Matlack: it was his 3,000th hit, something only 10 men before him had accomplished. It was also his last

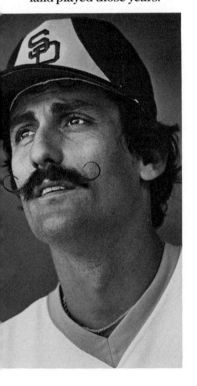

Rollie Fingers, one of baseball's all-time top relief pitchers. With Oakland during the World Championship years 1972, '73, and '74, he won 27 games in relief and saved 61 more. In addition, he relieved in 16 of the 19 World Series games Oakland played those years.

regular-season hit in the major leagues—because three months later, on December 31, New Year's Eve, at 9:22 P.M., a nervous Roberto Clemente—he never did like to fly—took off from San Juan aboard a rickety old DC-7, its cargo hold loaded with eight tons of food, clothing, and medical supplies. Instead of partying the New Year in, he was bringing desperately needed relief supplies from Puerto Rico to Managua, Nicaragua, devastated by an earthquake a week earlier. The plane never made it to Nicaragua. It practically never made it off the ground. One engine exploded almost immediately after takeoff, followed by further explosions, and the blazing DC-7 plummeted into the Atlantic Ocean barely a mile off the Puerto Rican coast. There were no survivors.

Roberto Clemente had been honorary chairman of the Nicaraguan Relief Committee. Honorary chairmen usually lend their name to a cause and then sit back and let others do the work. But Roberto Clemente was different. He died as he had lived, giving of himself, because he knew no other way.

Before Clemente's last season, a general players' strike—the first in baseball history—delayed the opening of the 1972 season for 10 days. The dispute centered on how much the club owners should contribute to the players' pension fund. So instead of discussion in March and April about Opening Day pitchers and the prospects for various teams, public attention was directed toward how much money the owners were offering, how many dollars the Players Association was demanding, and whether or not binding arbitration was an appropriate way to resolve the difference.

Hardly had the strike been settled, largely in the players' favor, before the U.S. Supreme Court ruled against outfielder Curt Flood in a suit he had brought against the baseball establishment. Flood had been traded by the Cardinals to the Phillies in late 1969, but he refused to report to Philadelphia even though he was offered a $100,000 contract. Instead, he sued to become a free agent, claiming that the "reserve clause"—making him the lifetime "property" of whatever club holds his contract—constituted involuntary servitude and was therefore unconstitutional. The Supreme Court, however, upheld the status quo, although conceding that the reserve clause was an "anomaly" in this day and age that Congress might well examine.

Omens for the later seventies: the Dollar Decade was on its way! Financial and legal expertise were becoming necessities for the **au courant** baseball fan.

In that connection, two dozen major leaguers were reportedly earning salaries of $100,000 or more in 1972, led by Henry Aaron ($200,000), Carl Yastrzemski ($167,000), Willie Mays

Tobacco-chewing Catfish Hunter, winner of more than 20 games every season from 1971 through 1975. In his rookie year, 1968, he pitched a perfect game against the Minnesota Twins, and in 1974 he was the Cy Young Award winner in the American League.

($165,000), and Roberto Clemente and Bob Gibson ($150,000 each). Incidentally, Aaron, Mays, Clemente, and Gibson all voted in favor of the strike at the start of the season. Yaz, on the other hand, did not.

On the field of play, gradually being pushed into the background by high finance, the Oakland Athletics were beginning to dominate baseball as no team had in two decades. Owner Charlie Finley's hirsute Athletics quarreled with him and feuded among themselves, but once they got on the ball field they knew what they were doing well enough to win three straight World Series—in 1972, '73, and '74. No other team had ever accomplished that except Joe McCarthy's Yankees in the late thirties (four World Championships) and Casey Stengel's Yankees in the early fifties (five World Championships).

Charlie Finley may have had trouble getting along with people, but he had an undeniable sixth sense when it came to building a winning ball team. The Oakland A's of the early seventies had outstanding pitching, a solid defense, and enviable power. On the mound were Catfish Hunter, Vida Blue, Ken Holtzman, Blue Moon Odom, and reliever Rollie Fingers. Behind the plate Ray Fosse and Gene Tenace; in the infield Mike Epstein and then Gene Tenace at first base, Dick Green at second, Bert Campaneris at shortstop, and Sal Bando at third; and Reggie Jackson, Bill North, and Joe Rudi in the outfield.

Pitching was the fulcrum of Oakland's success. Vida Blue won 20 or more games three times, with one no-hitter; Ken Holtzman was a consistent 17- to 20-game winner, with two no-hitters; Rollie Fingers, one of baseball's all-time top relievers, regularly appeared in around 70 games a season; and Catfish Hunter won over 20 games five times and once pitched a perfect game (in 1968). Late in 1974 Jim Hunter, an amiable, unpretentious North Carolinian, was involved in one of the more bizarre conflicts between owner Charlie Finley and his players. Finley refused to make certain payments to Hunter as contractually specified, whereupon Hunter appealed to arbitration and was declared a free agent by virtue of Finley's breach of contract. Catfish then signed a five-year contract with the Yankees for a package variously estimated as worth somewhere between $2.8 and $3.7 million.

At shortstop, Bert Campaneris, born in Cuba in 1942, sparked the team with his speed and competitive drive. Campaneris is generally thought of as a defensive wizard and a speedster with a light bat. And a star on the base paths he was: seven seasons stealing over 50 bases, six times league leader, over 600 lifetime stolen bases—the only men who have stolen more bases than

Shortstop Bert Campaneris.

Oakland's heroes in the 1972 World Series. Rudi's fielding saved the second game, and Tenace hit four home runs and drove in nine runs during the Series.

Joe Rudi.

Gene Tenace.

Joe Rudi's sensational leaping backhand catch against the left-field wall in the ninth inning of the second game of the 1972 World Series. (The drive was hit by Cincinnati third baseman Denis Menke.)

Nolan Ryan. At left, on June 1, 1975, after pitching his fourth no-hitter. Below, delivering his fastball, timed at 100.9 miles an hour.

Campaneris are Lou Brock, Ty Cobb, Eddie Collins, Max Carey, and Honus Wagner. But his bat was not all that light: one year he hit 22 home runs, and indeed in his very first major league game he hit two of them, a feat accomplished by only two others in baseball history.

In fact, Campaneris's versatility is hard to believe unless seen. To demonstrate it, on September 8, 1965, against the California Angels, he played all nine positions, one inning at each position. In the minor leagues in 1962 he pitched two innings, giving up one hit and one run, walking two, and striking out four. But what made it remarkable was that he pitched right-handed to right-handed batters and left-handed to left-handed batters!

Oakland's three consecutive World Series victories were achieved against three different National League teams—the Cincinnati Reds in 1972, the New York Mets in 1973, and the Los Angeles Dodgers in 1974.

Oakland's heroes in 1972 were left fielder Joe Rudi, whose ninth-inning sensational leaping backhand catch of a long drive off Denis Menke's bat saved the second game, and catcher-first baseman Gene Tenace, who drove in nine runs with eight hits, including four home runs.

Dick Green, Oakland second baseman. His sparkling fielding made him the Most Valuable Player of the 1974 World Series, despite the fact that he failed to get a base hit.

Henry Aaron, nineteen-year-old second baseman for the Jacksonville Braves in the Sally League in 1953.

In 1973 Oakland squeaked by the Mets in seven games, and although Met reliever Tug McGraw kept insisting "You Gotta Believe" until the very end, in the final analysis it was the bats of Joe Rudi, Bert Campaneris, and Reggie Jackson that turned skeptics into believers. Reggie, as usual, was superb under pressure. With the Mets ahead three games to two, and on the verge of victory, Jackson drove in four runs to lead Oakland to triumphs in the sixth and seventh games.

In this Series, Oakland owner Charlie Finley's strange behavior attracted as much attention as what was happening on the field when he fired substitute second baseman Mike Andrews

Henry Aaron in 1974.
Below, hitting record-
breaking home run number
715 on April 8, 1974. The
ball is a blur as it leaves the
bat.

Jim Rice.

Fred Lynn.

Luis Tiant.

Three reasons why the Boston Red Sox won the American League pennant in 1975. Jim Rice batted .309 and drove in over a hundred runs. Fred Lynn hit .331 and also batted in over a hundred runs. And Luis Tiant racked up 18 victories with an assortment of whirling-dervish deliveries befitting Merlin the Magician.

Boston catcher Carlton Fisk.

Tony Perez, longtime
Cincinnati first baseman,
who drove in 90 or more
runs every year from 1967
through 1977.

Carl Michael Yastrzemski, the Pride of New England, in 1978.

Johnny Bench in 1968, at the age of twenty.

Ballet's Rudolf Nureyev has a rival in baseball's Johnny Bench. Actually, he is leaping in pursuit of a wild throw that is permitting Billy Williams to cross the plate on an inside-the-park home run.

Johnny Bench in 1978.

after Andrews made two costly errors in the twelfth inning of the second game. Finley's players revolted, including Manager Dick Williams, many asking to be traded, and Commissioner Kuhn ordered Andrews reinstated. When he came up to pinch-hit in the fourth game, Andrews received a standing ovation. And at the end of the seventh game, instead of the usual statement of praise and happiness, Dick Williams announced his resignation as Oakland manager.

As a sidelight, Oakland's pitchers outhit New York's, three hits to two, even though the Oakland hurlers had not been to bat all season prior to the World Series. For 1973 was the year the American League instituted a new rule allowing a Designated Hitter to bat throughout the game for the pitcher. Intended to produce more hitting, it has been less than a resounding success in that respect, since the designated hitter's additional hitting is offset by the fact that an effective pitcher no longer has to be removed for a pinch hitter in the late innings of a close game.

Lynn Nolan Ryan also made headlines in 1973, breaking Sandy Koufax's single season strikeout record of 382 by fanning 383 for the California Angels. A 6-foot-2-inch 190-pound Texan, quiet, industrious, most at ease at home or out in the fields with his bird dogs, Nolan Ryan first came up with the New York Mets in 1966, when he was only nineteen years old. In one of baseball's most famous giveaways he was traded to the California Angels, where he blossomed as one of the greatest of all strikout pitchers, with a fastball electronically timed at 100.9 miles an hour (as compared with Bob Feller's 98.6 miles an hour).

The only pitcher in history to strike out over 300 batters in five different seasons, with four no-hit games to his credit—but often the league leader in wild pitches and bases on balls as well as strikeouts—only wildness prevented him from becoming a consistent 25- or 30-game winner.

In 1974 the Oakland Athletics won their third consecutive World Series by swamping the Los Angeles Dodgers, four games to one. Highlighting the Series was the brilliant fielding of Oakland second baseman Dick Green. But more important, 1974 was the year Henry Aaron tied and then surpassed Babe Ruth's 714 lifetime home runs.

Aaron had ended the 1973 season with 713, just one shy of Ruth's record. With pressure building up all winter, he unbeliev-ably tied the record with the very first swing of his bat in 1974. And four days later, at 9:07 P.M. on April 8, before a Monday night nationwide television audience, he hit record-breaking home run number 715 in Atlanta off Dodger left-hander Al Downing.

Second baseman Joe Morgan, the Most Valuable Player in the National League in both 1975 and 1976. In 1976 he hit 27 home runs, drove in 111 runs, **and** stole 60 bases.

Outfielder George Foster. In 1977 he had a .320 batting average, hit 52 home runs, and drove in 149 runs.

Henry Louis Aaron was born February 5, 1934, in Mobile, Alabama. At the time, George Herman Ruth was no doubt preparing to celebrate his thirty-ninth birthday (the following day, February 6) and getting ready to go to spring training for what would turn out to be his last season as a Yankee. The Babe had 686 home runs then; closest to him, with **less than half** Ruth's total, were Rogers Hornsby (300) and another Henry Louis, this one with the last name of Gehrig (299). At that time it was inconceivable that the Babe's lifetime total would ever be matched, and especially farfetched that a black man would be the one to do it—after all, blacks had **never** been allowed to play in either the National or the American League. Henry Louis Aaron would be thirteen years old before Jackie Robinson could put on a Brooklyn Dodger uniform.

Hank Aaron broke into the majors with Milwaukee in 1954, seven years after Jackie broke the color barrier, a reputed singles and doubles hitter who could steal bases. And, in fact, he did get over 2,200 singles, over 600 doubles, and stole over 200 bases in his twenty-three-year career. But he also hit home runs, not booming fly balls that soared above the stadium roof, like the Babe, but rising line drives that crashed into the seats. He hit 715 of them through April 8, 1974, and another 40 before retiring at the end of the 1976 season, for a lifetime total of 755.

Not an exceptionally big man, at 6 feet and 180 pounds, Aaron hit home runs the way he lived, in moderation, while the Babe was a man of excess, a glutton, both on and off the field. Hank never hit as many as 50 home runs a season, something Ruth did four times, but he clouted between 30 and 45 so consistently that he overtook the Babe by sheer tenacity and durability. Over his career, Aaron homered on average once every 16.4 times at bat, Ruth once every 11.8 times.

For whatever it may be worth, since they played in different eras and remembering that for his first four years Ruth was primarily a pitcher (and a very good one), here is a comparison of their lifetime batting records:

	Games	At Bat	Hits	Doubles
Henry Aaron (1954-1976)	3,298	12,364	3,771	624
Babe Ruth (1914-1935)	2,503	8,399	2,873	506

	Triples	Home Runs	Runs Scored	Runs Batted In
Henry Aaron	98	755	2,174	2,297
Babe Ruth	136	714	2,174	2,204

	Stolen Bases	Bases on Balls	Strike-Outs	Batting Average
Henry Aaron	240	1,402	1,383	.305
Babe Ruth	123	2,056	1,330	.342

Pete Rose in the early sixties.

Pete, Pete, Jr. (age two), and Cincinnati manager Sparky Anderson.

At third base in the late seventies.

Who else?

Interference or not? Boston catcher Carlton Fisk, his eye on the ball, collides with Cincinnati's Ed Armbrister while trying to field Armbrister's bunt in the tenth inning of the third game of the 1975 World Series. Umpire Larry Barnett ruled that no interference was involved.

Carlton Fisk's twelfth-inning home run wins the sixth game of the 1975 World Series for the Boston Red Sox. The ball caromed off the left-field foul pole — presumably the only reason it didn't go foul is because Fisk kept it in fair territory by vigorous body English as he watched its flight.

Oakland won the American League Western Division title again in 1975, for the fifth consecutive time, but in the play-offs they were clobbered by the Boston Red Sox in three straight games, thereby setting the stage for what many consider the most exciting World Series of all time: Boston vs. Cincinnati, 1975.

The Red Sox pennant drive was inspired by two sensational rookies and two equally sensational veterans: Jim Rice and Fred Lynn, the rookies, aged twenty-two and twenty-three respectively; and Luis Tiant and Carl Yastrzemski, the veterans, aged thirty-four and thirty-six respectively. Boston had Carlton Fisk catching; Carl Yastrzemski, Denny Doyle, Rick Burleson, and Rico Petrocelli in the infield; Dwight Evans and Bernie Carbo in the outfield besides Rice and Lynn; and Rick Wise, Bill Lee, Reggie Cleveland, and Roger Moret pitching in addition to Tiant.

Andy Messersmith.

Their 1975 dispute with management revolutionized the economic structure of baseball.

Dave McNally.

Outfielder Larry Hisle, one of the major beneficiaries of the Messersmith-McNally arbitration decision. He played out his $47,000-a-year contract with Minnesota in 1977, thereby becoming a free agent, and then signed for six years with Milwaukee for an estimated $525,000 a year.

Tobacco-chewing George Brett, Kansas City Royals' third baseman, led the American League with a .333 batting average in 1976. In the 1978 American League play-offs he hit three home runs in one game in a losing cause against the Yankees.

Mark Fidrych won 19 games and lost only 9 in his rookie year, 1976, with a Detroit team that lost more games than it won. His uninhibited approach to pitching increased attendance when he was scheduled to pitch by an estimated 500,000 paid admissions during the season.

Bill Madlock, National League batting champion in 1975 and 1976.

Chris Chambliss hitting the home run that won the 1976
American League pennant for the New York Yankees—in the
bottom of the ninth inning of the fifth and deciding game of
the play-offs against Kansas City. (The catcher is Buck
Martinez and the umpire Arthur Frantz.)

Outfielder Bobby Bonds, the only
player to hit 30 or more home runs
and steal 30 or more bases five
times. He did it in 1969, 1973,
1975, 1977, and 1978.

Pitcher Frank Tanana led the American League in shutouts in 1977.

Pitcher John Candelaria won 20 games and lost only 5 for the Pittsburgh Pirates in 1977.

The Cincinnati Reds, 108-game winners during the regular season, were now a truly impressive Big Red Machine, all but unbeatable except for a less-than-imposing pitching staff. With Johnny Bench catching; Tony Perez at first base, Joe Morgan at second, Dave Concepcion at short, and Pete Rose at third; and Ken Griffey, Cesar Geronimo, and George Foster in the outfield, the Reds appeared overstocked with future Hall of Famers. Don Gullett, Jack Billingham, and Gary Nolan were the main starting pitchers, with Rawly Eastwick and Will McEnaney as relievers.

Johnny Lee Bench, born in Oklahoma City on December 7, 1947, one-eighth Choctaw Indian, somewhat moody and introspective, may be the best catcher in the history of baseball. There are only a handful of rivals: Yogi Berra, Roy Campanella, Mickey Cochrane, Bill Dickey, and Gabby Hartnett. Slightly over 6 feet tall, about 200 pounds, Bench as soon as he broke into the majors attracted attention with his catching abilities—his catlike quickness in pouncing on bunts, his effortless 90-mile-an-hour throws to the bases, his nonchalant backhand pickup of balls in the dirt. He was recognized by his peers as the best receiver in the game before he had been up half a season. His hitting was frosting on the

Mike Schmidt.

The Phillies' Mike Schmidt and
Greg Luzinski. Schmidt led the
National League in home runs in
1974, 1975, and 1976. And
Luzinski hit 39 home runs and
drove in 130 runs in 1977, while
batting .309.

cake: six years with over 100 runs batted in, including 148 in 1970, two years with 40 or more home runs, on two occasions three home runs in a game. It was no surprise when he was named National League Rookie of the Year in 1968 or the league's Most Valuable Player in 1970 and 1972.

If Johnny Bench is a finely crafted Rolls-Royce, smooth, effortless, perfect, then Pete Rose is a souped-up Chevy convertible. Flashy, high-spirited, tough as nails, Peter Edward Rose is a throwback to the likes of Pistol Pete Reiser, Enos Slaughter, Jackie Robinson, Pepper Martin, Frankie Frisch, and, yes, Tyrus Raymond Cobb. An inch or so under 6 feet, 195 pounds, husky, barrel-chested, Rose plays every game as though he were a rookie trying to make the team—running full speed to first base after receiving a base on balls, sliding headfirst into the bases, willing to play any position in order to help the team.

Why **run** to first base after a base on balls? "The faster I get to first," Rose explained, "the faster I can get to second."

Pete Rose joined the Reds in 1963 as a twenty-one-year-old second baseman, was moved to left field a few years later to make room for Tommy Helms, then to right field, and finally to third base: at all four positions he was selected on the National League's All-Star team. He was National League Rookie of the Year in 1963; league batting champion in 1968, 1969, and 1973; Most Valuable Player in 1973; and the thirteenth player in history to achieve 3,000 hits—Roberto Clemente was the eleventh, in 1972; Al Kaline the twelfth, in 1974; and Pete Rose the thirteenth, in 1978. In 1978 he also tied Wee Willie Keeler's National League record—set in 1897—by hitting safely in 44 consecutive games, a feat surpassed in all of major league history only by Joe DiMaggio's 56-game hitting streak in 1941.

With all their talent, the Cincinnati Reds managed to just squeak past the Red Sox in the 1975 World Series. Surely no Series has ever been more exciting! It went the full seven games, with five decided by one run—and in four of the five the winning run crossed the plate in the ninth or a later inning. In six of the seven games a team that was trailing at some point in the game bounced back to win it.

After the Red Sox took the first game, Cincinnati came back to win the second, 3-2, with a two-run ninth inning rally. The Reds also won the third game, this time with a run in the bottom of the tenth. Contributing to Cincinnati's win was a controversial interference play that generated arguments for weeks afterward: in the tenth inning, Cincinnati's Ed Armbrister laid down a bunt attempting to sacrifice a man to second; Boston catcher Carlton

Greg Luzinski.

Relief pitcher Sparky Lyle, winner of the Cy Young Award as the best pitcher in the American League in 1977.

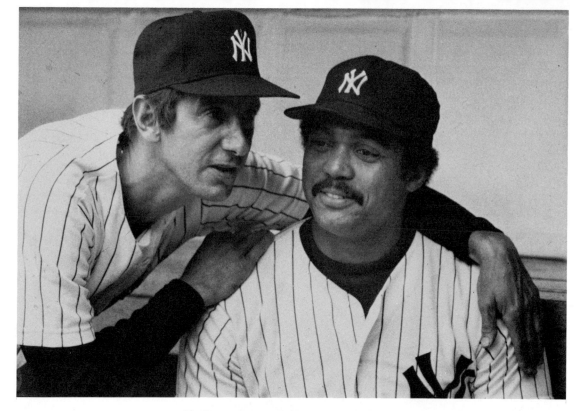

Yankee manager Billy Martin and Reggie Jackson in April 1977. It is
said that eventually the best of friends must part, and within two
months this honeymoon was definitely over as they almost came to
blows in the Yankee dugout while a nationwide television audience
watched in fascination. A year later their inability to coexist
contributed to Martin's midseason departure as Yankee manager.

Fisk collided with him while trying to get to the ball, and then
threw wildly to second. When the smoke cleared, there were Reds
on second and third. Boston's claim that interference by
Armbrister prevented Fisk from making the play was not allowed,
after which Cincinnati second baseman Joe Morgan singled to win
the game.

Game six, at Boston's Fenway Park on October 21, 1975, was
the all-time thriller. Cincinnati was leading in the Series, three
games to two, and the Red Sox had to win to stay alive. Fred Lynn
homered in the very first inning to put Boston ahead, 3-0. But the
Big Red Machine tied it up and then went ahead, 6-3. It looked like
the end of the trail for the Red Sox. In the bottom of the eighth,
however, with two out, Bernie Carbo pinch-hit a three-run
homer—his second pinch home run of the Series—and suddenly
the game was all tied up at 6-6. Boston then loaded the bases in the
ninth, but Cincinnati left fielder George Foster threw Denny Doyle
out at the plate to prevent the winning run from scoring. In the

Willie Stargell.

Willie Stargell, 6 feet 3 inches tall and 215 pounds, hit 20 or more home runs for Pittsburgh every year but one from 1964 through 1978. In 1971 he hit 48 homers and drove in 125 runs, in 1973 44 homers and drove in 119 runs. As Willie grew older, Dave Parker, 10 years younger, took up the slack: 6 feet 5 inches tall and 220 pounds, in 1977 Parker hit 21 home runs and led the National League in batting with a .338 average; and in 1978 he hit 30 homers, drove in 117 runs, and again led the league in batting with a .334 average.

Dave Parker.

eleventh, Joe Morgan smashed what looked like a sure home run, but Red Sox right fielder Dwight Evans made a sensational catch to keep the score tied. Finally, in the twelfth inning, Carlton Fisk won the game for Boston with a drive that caromed off the left-field foul pole; presumably the only reason the ball didn't go foul was that Fisk kept it in the park by body English as he watched its flight.

In the eleventh inning of this game Pete Rose came up to bat, turned to Red Sox catcher Carlton Fisk behind the plate, and said, "Wow, man, I don't know who'll win this, but isn't it great just to be here!"

In the seventh game, an anticlimax after the previous day's heroics, more than 75 million television viewers saw Boston take an early three-run lead. But Cincinnati tied it in the seventh inning and finally won the game and the World Series on a single by the ubiquitous Joe Morgan in the ninth inning.

Arguments about the interference play in the third game had barely died down before controversy suddenly flared up again—this time provoked by an arbitrator's decision that threatened to revolutionize the economic structure of the game. Pitchers Andy Messersmith of the Los Angeles Dodgers and Dave McNally, long-time Baltimore star, had played the 1975 season without signing their contracts. At the end of the season they declared themselves free agents. The owners, of course, invoked the reserve clause, which provided that a player remains bound to the club that has been holding his contract whether he signs for another year or not. Messersmith and McNally appealed to the Players Association and the dispute went to Arbitration under the terms of the Basic Labor-Management Agreement between the Players Association and the owners.

Curt Flood had attempted to break the reserve clause six years earlier by litigation in the courts, claiming it constituted in-voluntary servitude and was therefore illegal. In this instance, however, Messersmith and McNally were claiming not illegality but merely that it was part of a labor-management contract subject to adjudication under the terms of a collective bargaining agreement.

On December 23, 1975, arbitrator Peter Seitz announced his decision: a player who "plays out" his contract by not signing for a year has discharged his contractual obligations. Messersmith and McNally were free to sign with whomever they wished.

The Seitz decision resulted in a bitter collective-bargaining struggle between the players and the owners. The players claimed that clearly the decision applied to everyone and that there no longer was any such thing as a reserve clause. The owners claimed

Above, Reggie Jackson slides home safely as the ball eludes catcher Carlton Fisk's grasp. At right, Fisk goes to the mound to confer with relief pitcher Bill Campbell. Campbell won 13 games for the Red Sox in 1977 and saved another 31.

The date is October 18, 1977. Sixth game of the World Series: Yankees vs. Dodgers. Above, Reggie Jackson hits his third successive home run of the game, his fifth of the series, in the eighth inning. (The Dodgers' catcher is Steve Yeager and the umpire John McSherry.) At right, Yankee pitcher Mike Torrez has just caught pinch-hitter Lee Lacy's pop fly for the final out of the game and of the World Series.

the decision merely applied to two individuals, Messersmith and McNally, and had no general applicability. The owners also appealed to the courts to have the decision overturned, on the grounds that the reserve clause was not within the purview of the Basic Labor-Management Agreement with the Players Association, but without success.

When no agreement was reached between the Players Association and the owners by March 1, the traditional opening day for spring training, the owners locked the players out, refusing to open spring training facilities. However, at the first sign of progress in negotiations, on March 17, 1976, Commissioner Bowie Kuhn ordered spring training to begin while bargaining continued.

Lou Brock.

Lyman Bostock, twenty-seven years of age, fleet hard-hitting Angels' outfielder, was accidentally shot and killed on September 23, 1978. Bostock hit .323 in 1976 and .336 in 1977. One of the highest-paid players in baseball, he started slowly in 1978 and offered to return his April salary because he felt he didn't deserve it. When the Angels declined his offer, he proved it was no empty gesture by donating the money to charity. The good, it has often been said, die young.

Jim Palmer.

Steve Carlton.

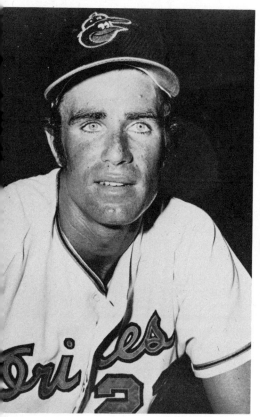

Two of the best pitchers in baseball in the seventies...some would say the two best. Jim Palmer won the Cy Young Award as the best pitcher in the American League three times—in 1973, 1975, and 1976. And Steve Carlton won it twice in the National League—in 1972 and 1977.

Steve Garvey, the smoothest-fielding and hardest-hitting first baseman in the
National League in the 1970s. He was voted the league's Most Valuable Player
in 1974.

Ron Guidry, minus his falling cap. But his cap was just about all he lost in
1978, when he won 25 games, lost only 3, and had a 1.74 earned run average.

By midyear the Players Association and the owners had agreed upon a new modified version of the reserve system: any player who wished could become a free agent after six years in the major leagues (and could demand to be traded after five years). As a transition measure, anyone playing without a signed contract through the 1976 season would become a free agent after that season, and the same for 1977. However, those who became free agents would not be **completely** free; a reentry draft would be held after each season and a free agent could only negotiate with a maximum of thirteen clubs that, in the reentry draft, had acquired the right to bargain with him.

Thus began the era of baseball millionaires. Dave McNally retired to Montana, but in April of 1976 Andy Messersmith was the first to reap the benefits as he signed a three-year contract with Atlanta for a reported $1 million. After the 1976 season, Reggie Jackson signed a five-year contract with the Yankees for about $3 million, and a dozen other brand-new free agents also signed multiyear million-dollar contracts. After the 1977 season another dozen free agents did the same, for amounts ranging up to and even slightly above $3 million. Newspaper readers found it increasingly difficult to distinguish between the sports pages and the financial section.

The bonanza was not confined to those who played out their contracts. Many negotiated million-dollar deals without switching clubs. Third baseman Mike Schmidt of the Phillies, for example, did not become a free agent but nevertheless signed a new six-year contract with the Phillies for close to $3.5 million. In 1977 Reggie Jackson was reportedly making an annual salary of $580,000, Mike Schmidt $560,000, Joe Rudi $420,000, Joe Morgan $400,000, and another two dozen or so were said to be getting somewhere between $300,000 and $400,000 a year.

Against this background of dollar signs, renewal options, and renegotiation bickering, and despite spring training lockouts, to everyone's surprise the 1976 season opened on schedule. The Cincinnati Reds won the National League Western Division title and the Philadelphia Phillies the Eastern Division, while in the American League it was Kansas City and the New York Yankees.

In the National League play-offs, the Big Red Machine, as awe-inspiring as in 1975, swept three straight from the Phillies even though Philadelphia had a power-packed lineup that included third baseman Mike Schmidt and left-fielder Greg Luzinski, as well as Steve Carlton with his third season of twenty or more victories.

Billy Martin's Yankees had a far more difficult time in the American League play-offs. New York finally edged out the Kansas

City Royals with a dramatic home run by first baseman Chris Chambliss in the bottom of the ninth inning of the fifth and deciding game.

The 1976 World Series was a walkover for Johnny Bench, Pete Rose, Joe Morgan, George Foster & Company. They had little trouble taking four in a row from the Yankees, with Bench almost single-handedly winning the fourth and final game with two home runs that accounted for five runs in a game where the Yankees got only two.

The following year, 1977, belongs to Reginald Martinez Jackson. Colorful, temperamental, impulsive, egotistical one moment and humility personified the next, Reggie Jackson, who was born in Wyncote, Pennsylvania, in 1946 and raised in a Philadelphia suburb by his father, a tailor, went to Arizona State University on a football scholarship before being induced by a $90,000 bonus to try his hand at professional baseball. Within two years he was in the big leagues, and two years after that, in 1969, he hit 47 home runs for the Oakland Athletics. In 1973 he was unanimously voted the American League's Most Valuable Player, after which he proceeded to get nine hits and drive in six runs in the 1973 World Series against the Mets.

After playing with Baltimore in 1976 without a signed contract, Jackson became a free agent and toward the year's end signed for five years and about $3 million with the Yankees. He received a higher offer from Montreal but chose the Yankees. "If I go to New York," he said, "maybe they'll name a candy bar after me."

From his triumphal arrival in New York early in 1977 straight through the World Series, Jackson was constantly in the headlines. The Yankees were a strong team but riddled with dissension, much of it centering in one way or another on Reggie Jackson. His low point of the year was reached on June 18, when he and manager Billy Martin almost came to blows in the Yankee dugout while a national television audience looked on in fascination. His high point was to come exactly four months later, on October 18.

The Yankees and Los Angeles Dodgers appeared to be rather evenly matched before the 1977 Series began. New York had Chris Chambliss at first base, Willie Randolph at second, Bucky Dent at short, and Graig Nettles at third, with Jackson, Mickey Rivers, Roy White, and Lou Piniella in the outfield. Thurman Munson did the catching, Ed Figueroa, Ron Guidry, Don Gullet, Catfish Hunter, Mike Torrez, and Sparky Lyle the pitching.

Los Angeles looked about as strong, with Steve Garvey at first base, Dave Lopes at second, Bill Russell at short, Ron Cey at third,

Graig Nettles can levitate without mirrors. The best fielding third baseman since Brooks Robinson, and the American League's home run leader in 1976, Nettles finally received the national acclaim he had long deserved when his superlative fielding turned the tide in favor of the Yankees in the 1978 World Series.

Catcher Thurman Munson tensely awaits both the ball and the base runner as they simultaneously approach at full speed. (The umpire is Ron Luciano.) A devastating clutch hitter, Munson batted .529 in the 1976 World Series, .320 in the 1977 Series, and .320 again in the 1978 Series. He was voted the American League's Most Valuable Player in 1976.

and Reggie Smith, Rick Monday, and Dusty Baker in the outfield. Steve Yeager did the catching, Burt Hooten, Tommy John, Rick Rhoden, and Don Sutton the pitching.

But those who thought the teams equally matched had not reckoned on what happens to Reggie Jackson's adrenaline when the chips are down. The Yankees won the Series in six games as Jackson hit .450 and smashed a record five home runs—three of them in the sixth and final game on October 18, with three successive swings of his bat. In fact, since he had homered in his last time up in the fifth game, and walked the first time up in the final game, Jackson actually hit four home runs in four consecutive official times at bat. Even George Herman Ruth, in all his World Series, had never reached such heights.

Even more historic in 1977 than Reggie Jackson's epic performance was Lou Brock's steal of his 893rd base on August 29—thereby breaking a record that only a few years before everyone had considered untouchable: Ty Cobb's 892 lifetime stolen bases. Slightly under 6 feet tall, 170 pounds, handsome, thoughtful, Louis

Clark Brock grew up in Collinston, Louisiana, one of nine children in a dirt-poor sharecropper family. On the basis of academic (not athletic) achievement, he made it to Southern University at Baton Rouge, where he was a mathematics major until a $30,000 bonus persuaded him to leave after his junior year.

In his early years Lou Brock was known as a long-ball hitter; indeed, he is one of the few who ever drove a home run into the center field bleachers at New York's Polo Grounds, over 480 feet from home plate. He gradually shifted gears, however, to concentrate on line-drive singles and doubles—then stretching them by stealing the next base. In 1974, when at the age of thirty-five Brock stole an amazing 118 bases, he broke Ty Cobb's old mark of 96 in the Cardinals' 134th game of the season, and Maury Wills's record of 104 in the 142nd game. No asterisk for Lou Brock!

As awesome as Brock was as a base runner, his performance when under pressure was no less impressive. In a total of 21 World Series games (in 1964, '67 and '68) he batted an extraordinary .391, with 21 singles, 7 doubles, 2 triples, and 4 home runs. He also stole 14 bases, drove in 13 runs, and scored another 16 himself.

The same four teams won their divisional titles in 1978 as in 1977—the Los Angeles Dodgers and Philadelphia Phillies in the National League and the New York Yankees and Kansas City Royals in the American League. The Dodgers, paced by Steve Garvey's four home runs, then trounced the Phillies in the play-offs for the National League Pennant—the third such defeat for Philadelphia in three years.

In the American League, fireworks exploded from beginning to end. It started with the Red Sox looking as though they would run away with everything, as the Yankees spent most of their early-season energy in a state of well-publicized turmoil stirred up by the clashing egos of manager Billy Martin, outfielder Reggie Jackson, and others. Martin resigned on July 24, after a particularly intemperate outburst in which he impugned the veracity of both Reggie and owner George Steinbrenner. The ensuing tranquillity under new manager Bob Lemon gave the New Yorkers a chance to pull themselves together, and they began to win consistently, ending the regular season in a tie with the Red Sox.

In a one-game play-off, the first tie-breaking play-off in the American League since 1948, Yankee shortstop Bucky Dent smashed a three-run homer in the seventh inning to sink Boston, 5-4. The Yankees thereby capped a comeback of historic proportions. They had been 14 games behind league-leading Boston

Rod Carew.

Rod Carew.

as late as July 19. The only other teams to ever make comparable comebacks had been the 1914 Boston Braves (15 games behind on the fourth of July) and the 1951 New York Giants (13½ games out of first place on August 11).

The Yankees followed this up by promptly beating the Kansas City Royals, three games to one, to take the American League pennant in a blaze of glory. Like the unhappy Phillies, it was the Royals' third play-off defeat in three years—which prompted some observers to suggest that it might be a good idea to match the Royals against the Phillies in an annual October consolation series (with the winner meeting the Boston Red Sox).

Nor were the never-say-die heroics of the New Yorkers at an end. They lost the first two games of the 1978 World Series to the Dodgers, thereby returning to their by-now-familiar position as underdogs. Evidently this was just what they needed, because they rebounded with a vengeance once again, sweeping the next four games from Los Angeles to take the World Championship, four games to two. The third game, the one that turned the tide in the Yankees' favor, was highlighted by the brilliant fielding of third baseman Graig Nettles. Thereafter, timely hitting by Reggie Jackson, Thurman Munson, Roy White, Lou Piniella and the rest of the batting order took over. For the Series as a whole, Reggie

Jackson hit .391, with 2 (more) home runs and 8 runs batted in; Thurman Munson hit .320 and drove in 7 runs; and, surprisingly, shortstop Bucky Dent and substitute second baseman Brian Doyle both hit well over .400.

But the come-from-behind Yankees were not the whole story in 1978. Rod Carew, for example, batted .333 to win his seventh American League batting title in 10 years. In a sense, 1978 was an off-year for Carew. The previous year he had flirted with .400 during most of the season and finally wound up hitting .388, the highest batting average since Ted Williams's identical figure 20 years earlier (and the second highest since Ted's .406 in 1941).

Rodney Cline Carew was born in Panama on October 1, 1945, and migrated to New York City with his mother and three sisters when he was sixteen years old. He was named Rodney Cline—not the most common Panamanian name—after an American doctor who helped deliver him when his mother unexpectedly gave birth while en route to the hospital. Six feet tall and 175 pounds, contemplative, fastidious, self-disciplined, Carew is as reserved a person as Reggie Jackson is flamboyant. So extraordinary is his batting artistry that it has tended to overshadow his base-stealing skills: in 1969 he stole home seven times, tying a record set by Pete Reiser in 1946.

Lou Brock, Rod Carew, Reggie Jackson! Are the stars of the seventies as good, as durable, as exciting as those of generations past? Of course they are: in addition to Brock, Carew, and Jackson, one has only to think of Johnny Bench, Joe Morgan, Jim Palmer, Dave Parker, Pete Rose, Tom Seaver, and Yaz.

Ty Cobb, the Babe, Honus, Matty, Walter Johnson—now they appear more legendary than ever. But as time passes so will today's stars as they, too, become enshrined in memory.

PICTURE CREDITS

We are deeply indebted to a number of people for their generous assistance in photo research and help in gathering the 554 photographs reproduced in this book. Our special thanks, for their many kindnesses, go to Jack Redding, Librarian of the National Baseball Hall of Fame and Museum in Cooperstown, New York; to Michael P. Aronstein, President of The Card Memorabilia Associates, Ltd., in Amawalk, New York; and to the many players and players' families who graciously permitted the use of pictures from their personal albums. The remaining photographs are from the following sources:

BETTMANN ARCHIVE: pp. 6, 10 bottom, 21 bottom left, 30 left, 45 bottom, 235 top right.

ROBERT C. BARTOSZ, Pennsauken, N.J.: pp. 271, 346 left.

BROWN BROTHERS, Sterling, Pa.: pp. 5 bottom, 11, 13 bottom, 48, 51, 62.

CULVER PICTURES: pp. 29, 35, 52 bottom, 53 top, 59 right, 69 right, 103, 143 right.

RONALD C. MODRA, Port Washington, Wis.: pp. 281 right, 319, 320, 321, 322 bottom, 325 bottom, 329 top left, 329 top right, 329 bottom, 330 top, 331, 334, 336 right, 339 top, 342 bottom, 343 top right, 348, 350 top, 350 bottom, 356, 362-63, 366, 367.

NEW YORK DAILY NEWS: pp. 240, 241 top left, 250 top, 308 top and bottom.

PHOTOWORLD: pp. ix, 9 bottom, 67 bottom left, 231, 269.

LOUIS REQUENA, Little Ferry, N.J.: pp. 272, 280 top and bottom, 285 top, 293, 300, 303, 304, 306, 307, 315 top and bottom, 323 top, 323 bottom, 330 bottom, 336 left, 339 bottom, 342 top left, 342 top right, 343 bottom, 344 top, 344 bottom right, 345, 346 right, 349, 352, 353, 354, 355, 358, 359, 364.

UNITED PRESS INTERNATIONAL: pp. 3, 74, 152, 194, 205 bottom right, 218, 219, 237 top, 259 top right, 261, 265, 285 bottom, 287 right, 290 top right, 316, 325 top, 340, 341, 357 top.

WIDE WORLD PHOTOS: pp. 235 bottom, 236 bottom, 275 top right, 278 top, 278 bottom, 282 bottom, 287 left, 297 bottom, 314 bottom, 317, 328 bottom.

INDEX

NOTE: Page numbers in boldface refer to illustrations.